ONE HIT
WONDER

THE JIMMY GLASS STORY

ONE HIT WONDER

THE JIMMY GLASS STORY

JIMMY GLASS
WITH ROGER LYTOLLIS

TEMPUS

First published 2004

Tempus Publishing Limited
The Mill, Brimscombe Port,
Stroud, Gloucestershire, GL5 2QG
www.tempus-publishing.com

British Library Cataloguing in Publication Data.
A catalogue record for this book is available from the British Library.

ISBN 0 7524 3181 1

Typesetting and origination by Tempus Publishing Limited
Printed and bound in Great Britain

CONTENTS

ACKNOWLEDGEMENTS

Many thanks to the following people for advice, information and encouragement: Andy Baker, Daniel Balado-Lopez, Richard Banyard, Johnny Becker, Holly Bennion, Martin Brodetsky, Loftus Brown, Andy Burton, Patrick Collins, Rachel Cugnoni, Hunter Davies, Tony Dobson, Firmo, Mike Gardner, Peter Hill, James Howarth, Chris Jackson, Ali Kazemi, Elaine Little, Andy Lyons, Gareth Moore, Peter Phillips, Phil Rigby, Rob Sharman, Mike Ticher, Neil Witherow and all at Table One.

Also to Mam and Dad, Anna, Kat, Rosie, Lou, Jason and Rachel, Eve and Hannah.

Roger Lytollis
Cumbria, August 2004

FOREWORD
by Patrick Collins

It was a few minutes before five o'clock on the afternoon of 8 May 1999 and my 800-word article was almost written. It was a sad story, made all the more melancholy by the sight of grown men beginning to weep. The match was in its final seconds when Carlisle won a corner. 'Hallo,' said my friend from the *Sunday Telegraph*, 'the 'keeper's coming up for it.'

There are small children in Carlisle who can tell you in gleeful, graphic detail precisely what happened next. Graham Anthony took the kick and swung it on to the head of Scott Dobie. The header was parried on the line by the Plymouth Argyle goalkeeper, James Dungey, but the ball ran loose and fell at the feet of his opposite number.

Jimmy Glass swung his right boot, made thumping contact and stood rooted in disbelief as the ball billowed the net. Carlisle United's seventy-one-year existence in the Football League had been breathlessly preserved. The threat of extinction had been averted. Brunton Park was going gloriously insane. The entire pitch was awash with ecstatic humanity. And my computer screen was littered with 800 words of complete irrelevance.

Fifteen minutes later, the obituary had become a eulogy to the unknown goalkeeper. The last kick of the season had produced its most memorable story, and I doubt that the old game has come up with a better one in the years since '99.

When the crowd released him, Jimmy came to speak to the press. He was 'dead pleased for the lads'. He wasn't sure of his immediate future 'at this moment in time'. Why had he moved into attack? ''Cos there's always goals in the six-yard box'. And we scribbled it down as if he were disclosing the mysteries of the universe. That's what happens when you save football clubs from extinction.

In truth, I had barely heard of Glass before his heroic spasm. In common with two or three journalists, I had travelled up from London to record the downfall of a decent club. I was also prepared to pour a little scorn upon the Carlisle chairman, the preposterous Michael Knighton. Just a day before that critical match, Knighton had boasted that Carlisle had made a profit of £1.4m in the previous season. This owed something to the fact that they had sold players to the value of £2.12m while spending just £100,000. Naturally, the fans chanted all manner of imaginative abuse at the chairman throughout the first half of the match and, far from deploring their bawdy candour, a good many members of the press joined in. It was utterly disgraceful, and rather wonderful.

But Knighton was not the story; indeed, he was scarcely more than a footnote. Jimmy Glass was the real tale, and I had no idea just how extraordinary a tale he was until I read this remarkable book.

If you really want to know how it felt to be a member of football's poor bloody infantry in the 1990s then you will find it in the career of Jimmy Glass. He enters his career with confidence, certainty and breezy optimism, and he discovers that the game has a way of challenging and undermining all those virtues. He suffers rejection and humiliation, his illusions are corroded by the bitterness of experience, he acquires a gambling habit which devours and almost destroys him. And he relates it all with a chilling frankness and the eye of an uncommon observer.

He understands that his life was changed by that fleeting moment on the afternoon of 8 May 1999. Now, with sensitive perception, he tries to understand those changes.

I recall the bewildering drama of that afternoon, how we tried to record events, how we raced to the station to catch the last train to London. As the miles slid away, my friend from the *Sunday Telegraph* congratulated himself: 'D'you remember me telling you that Jimmy Glass was coming up for the corner?' he asked. 'You never mentioned Jimmy Glass,' I said. 'You said "the 'keeper". You didn't even know his name.' He thought for a moment, then graciously agreed. 'All right,' he said, 'I didn't know his name. But I do now. And so does everyone else.'

Patrick Collins,
chief sports writer for The Mail on Sunday,
July 2004

INTRODUCTION

In some ways, football has changed beyond recognition since I signed my first professional contract with Crystal Palace in 1991. Palace finished third in the old First Division that year, 10 points above Manchester United. That couldn't happen now. I want this book to show how the goalposts have been moved to protect big clubs and stop smaller clubs getting above their station. These days, 'doing a Wimbledon' means uprooting from your home and alienating your supporters.

English football doesn't just mean the Premiership. You don't have to be at Old Trafford or Highbury to see the passion football generates. It happens every Saturday in Hartlepool and Torquay. But if the dice keep being loaded in favour of the elite, many of these smaller clubs will disappear. This is a war cry to the fans: do you want ninety-two League clubs? Or are you happy to buy the Manchester United brand? Someone in football needs to speak out, and you can bet it won't be Premiership players while the game is handing them £20,000-plus a week.

So here I am. During the past decade I've experienced nearly every level of football: the Premiership, Divisions One, Two and Three, the Conference, the Dr Martens League, the Vauxhall-Opel League, the Jewson Wessex League, the Bournemouth Sunday league. I've played against David Beckham three times. I've been involved in an FA Cup semi-final and I've played at Wembley. I've only scored one goal, but you can't have everything.

My time in football was the most momentous period the game has seen. Division One became the Premiership and sport became business. The Bosman ruling and the influx of foreign players changed English football dramatically, for better and for worse.

Through all these changes the only constant factor has been the fans. This book is for them, especially those who have seen their clubs brought close to collapse by chairmen, players and football's authorities.

The book highlights a lot of mistakes by organisations and individuals. Many of the mistakes are mine. I hope I've learned something, and that the people with the power to make a difference to football have as well. And I hope my story is entertaining, because that's what this wonderful game should be all about.

Jimmy Glass
Dorset, June 2004

'There can't be long left. We're well into stoppage time.

We need a goal… it's now or never, as the song says.

Now or never, do or die. We've GOT to score.

Come on, lads! Make it happen!

Come on! Get a cross in – GO ON!

Deflection… this is it then – a corner. *This must be our last chance.*

Should I go up for it? Might as well. I can't do much back here.

If I go up I could be the one who makes it happen.

Imagine if I scored! I'd be the hero!

Or I could fall on my arse and be a laughing stock.

Sod it, I have nothing to lose but my dignity.

Here I go… listen to the crowd!

This is what they want – something to get excited about!

Wait – don't take the corner yet!

Give me a chance to reach the penalty area!

Okay, made it. Now, where should I run?

I'll go to the near post. Right, here it comes…

oh great – he's hit it straight to their full-back!

Shit – now I've got to get back to my goal.

I don't know if I can manage another hundred yards.

Please don't score! That would be so embarrassing…'

Bournemouth goalkeeper Jimmy Glass
runs upfield for a last-minute corner in the FA Cup third-round match,
Huddersfield Town v. Bournemouth, 13 January 1998

One

ON THE LADDER

Home was a semi-detached house in Worcester Park, where south-west London meets Surrey. My dad, Frank, was a policeman so I was never one to run riot. The closest I came to juvenile delinquency was a mouthful of Martini at a police disco. The organisers threatened to tell Dad and my life of crime was over.

I was born in 1973. My brother Paul is three years older. I'm a bit more flash and streetwise than he is, partly because of my upbringing in football. Paul doesn't like the game. He could easily have felt left out during our childhood because Dad loves it. But Paul concentrated on his studies, then he got married and went his own way.

Our younger brother, Iain, has touched my life more than anyone else. I was six when Iain was born. He didn't come into the world as a bouncing bundle of joy: he was born with spina bifida. Iain has never been able to walk, dress himself or take care of himself in any way. Every morning Mum takes him to his day centre then he comes home to watch TV in his room. He loves watching football. Iain has been ill several times. He has been close to death but has always pulled himself back. He desperately wants to stick around.

Iain changed us all. I spent my childhood thinking I would never have a life of my own. I would never get married or have a family because I owed it to Iain to look after him. Eventually I realised I owed it to him to live as full a life as possible. Mum and Dad became very protective. They devoted their lives to caring for Iain and shielding him from the world. My mum, Sheila, is one of the most amazing people I've ever met. I don't know how she copes with Iain. We've never discussed it. My parents had to accept Iain's condition and get on with things. I couldn't do it. I found it impossible to understand why my little brother will never fall in love, never have sex, never bring up a family.

Iain affected me more than he'll ever know. There's a lot of anger inside me and every so often it bursts out through rash behaviour, like gambling away a month's wages or losing the plot with people. Throughout my football career I always looked at the players around me to see if they were using their ability – to see if they were taking the chances Iain never had. If I saw someone who wasn't trying I'd fly into a rage. Football clubs frustrated me for the same reason as players. I wanted clubs to fulfil their potential so I could fulfil mine. I wanted to become the perfect footballer. But instead of trying to get the best out of others, I should have concentrated on my own career.

The best footballers don't get distracted by events around them. The difference between them and me was Iain. Because my little brother was in a wheelchair, I was very frustrated. If things weren't right I wanted them changed. For a long time that was the driving force behind a lot of things in my life.

My first love was Liverpool FC. I was a diehard Reds fan until the age of eight, when I woke up one morning and became a diehard Tottenham fan. My hero was Liverpool and England goalkeeper Ray Clemence. When he switched his allegiance to Tottenham in 1981, so did I. Around the time Ray started playing for Spurs, I made my goalkeeping debut for 4th Worcester Park Cub Scouts. The urge to score goals as well as prevent them soon began to surface. I played as a striker for the last year and scored eight times in one match. My school stuck me in goal. Even back then I was never sure which end of the pitch I should be at.

In 1984 I moved to Richard Challoner Boys' School in Kingston, Surrey. My first girlfriend, Sasha, was at the girls' school down the road. We had an on-off relationship in which she had to compete with my passion for sport. I played every game I could: rugby, tennis, basketball and football. I was a central defender for the school football team. I made a point of not telling anyone that I was a goalkeeper because I didn't want to be tied to one position.

Losing was always unbearable, whatever position I played in. If my team was beaten in a playground kickabout I'd storm off in a huff. A P.E. teacher once told me: 'Throughout your life you'll hear people say, "It's not the winning that matters, it's the taking part." Well, bollocks to that.'

On Sundays I played in goal for a friend's team called Raynes Park Rovers in West Surrey Boys' League. We were rubbish. From a goal-keeper's point of view the only good thing about conceding ten goals every week is that you get plenty of practice. I may have let in ten but I stopped another twenty. One of the teams in our league was managed by a Chelsea scout called Keith Nimmo. After watching me play a few times he invited me to train with Chelsea's schoolboys. Every professional football club has schoolboys on their books. These lads train once or twice a week with the club's youth coaches. The club has first refusal on them when they turn sixteen and become eligible for an apprenticeship.

I couldn't wait to tell my friends that I was training with Chelsea. Their schoolboys trained on Tuesday nights at Battersea Park in south London. I turned up for my first session wearing my replica England goalie top and shorts. This was long before Chelsea was bought by a Russian billionaire. These days the club's schoolboys probably train on a bed of freshly plucked rose petals. Things were more primitive back in 1987. We trained on the same surface tennis players use for clay-court tournaments – concrete topped by clay and ash. When I'm in goal I dive around like a lunatic, but not on concrete. I trained at Battersea Park for nine weeks before a coach called me into his office. 'You're not what we're looking for,' he said. It seemed strange considering he'd never seen me play on grass.

Raynes Park Rovers were soon under new management: that of my dad. He had played football for the police and used to manage his station's team. Dad took his new role very seriously. He photocopied coaching manuals, found us a good training pitch and attracted better players. He was determined to avoid any accusations of favouritism towards his son: if one of our players was injured, Dad would rush to help him; if I was hurt he'd yell at me to get up. A referee once asked him to stop bollocking me: 'Frank – leave your son alone!'

Another team in our league was managed by a Crystal Palace scout called Vic Pennington. Before Dad took over Raynes Park Rovers, Vic's team had beaten us 10-0. Shortly after Chelsea rejected me Vic invited me to train with Palace's schoolboys. I must be one of the few goal-keepers to impress a scout who has seen him concede ten goals.

Crystal Palace was my local Football League team. They played at Selhurst Park, near Croydon, only half an hour from home. Even so, I'd never seen them. I'd never watched any live football because I was too busy playing. I trained with Palace's schoolboys one night a week at the club's training ground in Mitcham, south London. They played on grass, so that was an improvement. The only other goalkeeper was Michael Sullivan, whose older brother Neil went on to play in goal for Wimbledon, Tottenham and Scotland. Most of our coaching was done by one of Palace's YTS goalkeepers, Andy Woodman. There was nothing very technical but at least I was with a professional club.

After a few months, early in 1988, Palace asked me to sign school-boy forms. Mum and Dad took me to Selhurst Park for the first time to meet the club's manager, Steve Coppell. Coppell had been a brilliant midfielder for Manchester United and England before injury ended his career at the age of twenty-eight. He became Palace manager in 1984 and had led the club to several top-six finishes in the old Second Division. I was impressed with Coppell from the outset. He's a quiet, intelligent man who put me at ease and inspired confidence and loyalty. 'Football is a ladder,' he said, 'and you've just stepped onto the first rung.' I put pen to paper and Coppell gave us a guided tour of the ground. He also gave me a tracksuit in the club's colours: red and blue. I belonged.

My new status gained me tickets to Palace's first-team games. I was usually playing on Saturdays, but I went to Tuesday night matches with Dad. I knew next to nothing about the world I was watching. To me, professional football was all superstars, glitz and glamour. I sometimes wore my club tracksuit and hoped people would mistake this lanky fourteen-year-old for a professional player. Palace held open days when local schoolchildren were shown around. I was thrilled whenever they asked for my autograph. Then one day I saw the window cleaner surrounded by kids, signing his name for them.

My association with a professional club meant I was suddenly in demand. Life became a succession of football matches. On Saturdays I played in goal for a Sutton youth club called Centre 21. We were the best team in our league. We beat one team 28-0 at home and 24-0 away. I scored one of the goals when I ran upfield from my area. On Sundays I played for Raynes Park Rovers, but now as a forward. Dad always thought I was better as a striker than a goalkeeper. In one match I was marked by Chris Perry, who went on to play for Tottenham. I knocked the ball past him, accelerated away and slammed it into the net. Maybe Dad was right about my best position. I still didn't regard myself as an out-and-out goalkeeper because playing up front was just as rewarding. On Mondays and Thursdays I trained at Palace and on Wednesdays I played in goal for a youth team called Horley, whose manager was a Palace scout. When I got home every night at ten o'clock there was just time to grab something to eat before crashing into bed. Tuesday and Friday nights were the only time available for schoolwork. At fourteen, I had already made a choice that would affect the rest of my life. I had gambled my future on football.

Fourteen months after I became a Palace schoolboy, the club had to decide which of the lads in my year would get a YTS apprenticeship and which would find that the gamble on football had not paid off. I spent weeks dreading the night in April 1989 when we would learn our fate. The time finally came and I waited with Dad outside youth-team manager Alan Smith's office. One by one the boys who had been my teammates went in and came out. Some were smiling; others were in tears. Then it was my turn. I felt so proud when Alan offered me a YTS contract – two years as an apprentice goalkeeper. Two years to prove myself. Out of thirty boys in my year only seven were kept on. Michael Sullivan was rejected. He forced a smile and said, 'Well done.' At sixteen, his career was over.

I left school that June and started full-time at Palace a few weeks later. The money wasn't great: even back then you couldn't do a lot with £29.50 a week. But a foot in the door of a professional football club was priceless. Thank God I didn't have to fall back on my qualifications. It had been difficult to concentrate on schoolwork with an apprenticeship dangling and I had only passed two GCSEs, P.E. and drama, because I enjoyed them most. Ten years later a journalist would write that P.E. and drama was an appropriate combination for me.

It was a good time to be at Crystal Palace. The club had just been promoted to the old First Division – later to become the Premiership – for the first time in eight years. They had got there by beating Blackburn in the play-off final. In those days the final was played over two legs instead of a one-off match at Wembley or Cardiff. Blackburn had won their home leg 3-1. Palace were leading 2-0 in the second leg, which meant they would be promoted because they had scored an away goal. In the last minute of the match, Palace striker Ian Wright scored again to seal the club's return to the big time. There was a massive pitch invasion by the home supporters. I can only claim youth as my defence, but for a long time whenever I heard the words 'some people are on the pitch, they think it's all over – it is now!' I thought they were referring to the Palace fans that night at Selhurst Park.

My football career started in style, with a trip to Portugal for a youth-team tournament. Andy Woodman played in all the matches. We trained in the mornings then relaxed on the beach. What a great life!

Back home, I found that being an apprentice footballer was anything but glamorous. This realisation hit me when I was on my knees, scrubbing the training-ground toilets. When sixteen-year-olds go straight from school into professional football their egos can run away with them; the apprentice system was designed to keep their feet on the ground. It was also cheap labour. Every apprentice had a job and mine was cleaning the toilets. Each of us also looked after the boots and kit of three professionals. Mine included Alan Pardew, who went on to become the manager of Reading and West Ham.

Our day started at nine o'clock when we polished the boots we'd cleaned the previous afternoon. We got our three players' kit together and left it in their dressing room, then we carried the balls and goals onto the training pitch. We trained at the same time as the professionals, then we collected the balls, goals and kit and cleaned our players' boots. The pros got very stroppy if things weren't just right. Plenty of apprentices were bollocked for not warming their players' kit on a radiator, and pros are very particular about their boots. Ian Wright insisted on having his tongues flipped forward. Mark Bright once gave an apprentice a hiding for wearing his boots without permission.

Wright and Bright were Palace's star players. Wright was loud and aggressive; Bright was more reflective. Together they were an explosive strike partnership, which spread confidence throughout the club. Wrighty had passion and Steve Coppell knew how to channel it. Coppell drilled him hard every day on the training ground and helped make him a world-class striker who went on to play thirty-three times for England. The other pros included Mark Dennis, a veteran defender who was known as the hardest man in football. He'd been sent off countless times and was rumoured to have as many fights off the football field as on it. That side of him rarely surfaced on the training ground, though. He came in one day and said, 'My dad threw me an orange last night. I caught and peeled it with my left foot.' He was less complimentary about one of his fellow professionals: 'His first touch goes further than I can kick a ball.'

While the likes of Ian Wright and Mark Dennis were top dogs, we apprentices were left in no doubt about our place in the food chain. The youth team, the reserves and the first team each had their own dressing room, and you didn't venture above your station without a good reason. When a professional said 'Wash my car', you washed his car. Anyone who complained was told: 'We had to do it when we were apprentices.' The previous generation had had to sweep terraces and they never tired of telling us that we had it easy in comparison. I didn't really mind doing menial tasks. To a sixteen-year-old football fan, washing Ian Wright's car felt like an honour. The prevailing attitude today is that apprentices shouldn't do that kind of thing because their job is playing football. I never saw any problem with sweeping a floor or cleaning a few boots. It was an important lesson in the art of getting your head down and doing things you don't really fancy.

But at Palace, in common with most English clubs, there was too much emphasis on hard work and not enough on skill. Workhorses made it through the system because they did what they were told. Most 'flair' players were lost to the game, which is one reason why English football had become so unattractive by the end of the 1980s.

The English game had been stagnating since the 1966 World Cup win. Hooliganism had driven down attendances. English clubs were banned from European competitions after thirty-nine people were killed when Liverpool and Juventus fans fought at the 1985 European Cup final. When I signed YTS forms for Palace, ninety-five people had just died during an FA Cup semi-final at Hillsborough. Stadiums were old and decrepit. English football was characterised by complacency and a refusal to accept that the game elsewhere had moved on and left us behind.

At Palace the culture was stranded in the days, and the nights, of George Best. Many of our professional athletes spent their evenings at the Blue Orchid club in Croydon. Next morning they'd have a story about falling over in the street or getting locked out by the wife. They'd shuffle out of the dressing room at half past ten and train with a hangover for two hours. At half past twelve it was a race to see who could be first into the shower. Those who were more switched on would stay and do extra, but most would be away by one o'clock. As long as the booze was run off it was all right by the establishment. I never heard any coach or manager lay down the law about drinking. Some coaches knocked back more than the players. They had been brought up to drink and that's how they taught the next generation.

We continued the cycle. At my first apprentices' Christmas party, players were throwing up over the bar. By the end of the night no one could stand. It wasn't that players didn't care. Most of them were passionate about football. But drinking was as much part of being a footballer as kicking a ball. What did it matter if we were out on the piss when we knew the team we were facing on Saturday would be doing exactly the same?

If players were unprofessional, they were only following the example of their clubs. Palace's training ground was like something out of a Dickens novel. The dressing rooms were in an ancient wooden shack with cold concrete floors. It's no surprise that players weren't keen to stay behind and do more work in the afternoons: the reward for extra training was a freezing-cold shower. Anyone who turned on the taps after one o'clock would find there was no hot water left.

There was no limit to the penny-pinching. At the start of every season, each player was given two sets of kit. These were soon full of holes because they were so cheap. Each player had a squad number which was printed on every item of their kit. Before long the numbers fell off and it was every man for himself. In winter I often found one of the first-team squad wearing my tracksuit bottoms. Andy Gray, who was a star of the first team, once ran onto the training pitch in a sheepskin coat – when he'd arrived there had been no kit left. The club bought a load of cheap orange and green fluorescent bibs which looked like cast-offs from British Rail. You had international footballers training every day in bibs whose previous home may well have been a railway tunnel. And despite everything, Palace were one of the most successful teams in England. They did well because most other clubs were run in the same slipshod way.

The power behind Palace's throne was the club's chairman, Ron Noades. He made his money in the construction industry and became Wimbledon's chairman shortly before they were elected to the Football League in 1977. Four years later, while still running Wimbledon, he bought a controlling interest in Crystal Palace. The

League was worried about a conflict of interest so it ruled that no football club official could be involved with another club. Noades eventually sold Wimbledon and took charge at Palace. Incidents like this
helped give him a reputation as a wide boy. I once read a quote by the
chairman of Tooting & Mitcham, where Palace's reserve team played.
He said of Ron Noades, 'I was counting my fingers after shaking hands
with him.' However, it has to be said that Noades did a good job for
Crystal Palace. For example, he was the first chairman to see Steve
Coppell's potential and give him his first job in management.

Once a week, the YTS lads went to college in Croydon for a City &
Guilds course in sport and leisure, which included such diverse topics
as first aid and basketball. We strolled around acting as if we owned the
place. One time it snowed and the whole college bombarded us with
snowballs. The rest of the week our training sessions started at ten
o'clock when we warmed up by jogging around the pitch a few times.
There was no goalkeeper coaching. Most of my training was the same
as the outfield players': a bit of running, then some five-a-side or
seven-a-side matches. Players were never divided into defenders,
midfielders and forwards with specialist coaching for each position.
Alan Smith was usually the only coach for sixteen YTS lads, so it was
hard for him to cater for everyone.

Unlike the other apprentices I didn't have the chance to learn by
playing matches. Andy Woodman was a first-year professional goalkeeper, but he was eligible to play another year in the youth team
because his birthday was in August. At least I got to train with the first
team a couple of times a week. Steve Coppell loved my enthusiasm and
I was one of only two first-year apprentices who he regularly invited to
work with the first team. They already had two goalkeepers so I would
play as a striker. I could hold off defenders, whip in crosses and score
with both feet. I just found it so easy to put the ball in the net.
Forwards would sometimes go a whole morning without scoring
once, then they'd get in their car and go home quite happy. I always
thought Steve Coppell should have said to his strikers, 'If he can score
five goals, why can't you?' But people just laughed.

I thought they should have given me a few matches up front for the
youth team. Not many sixteen-year-olds can score goals against First
Division defenders. The fact that I was a goalkeeper makes it even

more ridiculous that my ability wasn't highlighted. Palace weren't playing me in goal, so why not give me a chance as a striker? But it never happened. The term 'frustrated forward' is truer in my case than in anyone's.

Despite my own lack of coaching, I had to train Palace's schoolboy 'keepers two nights a week, just as Andy Woodman had trained me. It was the only coaching they had, God help them. At the age of sixteen I had great difficulty in distinguishing my arse from a hole in the ground. The idea that I should be the one to explain the complexities of goalkeeping wasn't a great one, for them or me. Bob White, Palace's youth development officer, would ask: 'Can you coach the keepers tonight?' – except it wasn't really a question. I had to hang around all day at the training ground until they arrived at five o'clock, wondering what to teach them when I knew so little myself. I showed them what I'd been taught by Andy Woodman. Sometimes Palace's first-team keeper, Perry Suckling, came along to help. Perry was very enthusiastic, and that rubbed off on me. However, his love of football took a battering only a few weeks into my apprenticeship. I was listening to the radio the night it happened. Palace had been playing at Liverpool:

'We have a shock result from Anfield...'

'Christ!' I thought. 'We've only gone and beaten Liverpool!'

'Liverpool 9, Crystal Palace 0.'

Not surprisingly, that damaged Perry's confidence, and he left at the end of the season.

Soon after the Liverpool match we bought Nigel Martyn from Bristol Rovers. Suddenly I was understudy to Britain's first £1 million goalkeeper. Until then, Palace had been fairly cautious when it came to buying players, but Steve Coppell had spotted Nigel's potential and Ron Noades backed him. A million pounds turned out to be a good investment. Nigel was only twenty-three. He had a very silly moustache which didn't survive a season of piss-taking. Steve Coppell liked his decisiveness. When Nigel makes a decision he sticks with it, for better or worse. Nigel is a really decent man. He gave me bits of advice here and there but he probably saw me as a kid, like I did with young 'keepers later on.

By December 1989 I was feeling pretty pissed off about my lack of matches. I spoke to the YTS supervisor who visited football clubs to make sure the apprentices were okay. I explained how I'd been led to believe that playing the odd football match would be part of my duties at Crystal Palace Football Club. He had a chat with Bob White and the next thing I knew I was on loan at Dulwich Hamlet. Dulwich were in the Vauxhall-Opel Premier League, two levels below the old Fourth Division. The club call themselves 'The Pride of South London' – a claim the advertising standards people might like to investigate.

Dulwich used to be a big club in non-League terms but they had become run down over the years. They played at Champion Hill Stadium on the exotically named Dog Kennel Hill. Champion Hill was a massive concrete bowl. Crowds of 20,000 used to attend non-League internationals there; forty years on, Dulwich were lucky to get 300. The terraces were crumbling and covered in weeds. The dressing room wasn't much better. The showers were more like sprinklers.

The Pride of South London were bottom of the league and desperate for a goalkeeper. They must have been to chuck a sixteen-year-old in. My debut in senior football came one January afternoon in 1990 at Grays Athletic in Essex. During the warm-up I noticed Grays' big lump of a centre forward. No one within a two-mile radius could miss him. He looked quite intimidating, so I decided to set my stall out early. In the first minute I came for a cross and kneed him in the back. He was on the floor for ten minutes. My new teammates took quite a liking to me after that. In the next match I dived on the ball and someone volleyed me in the mouth. I spent the next week pushing my front teeth backwards and forwards with my tongue. Welcome to the beautiful game.

I trained at Palace and only turned up at Dulwich for matches. It felt like quite a high standard of football, but it wasn't really much better than Sunday league. I'm convinced we played at the same away ground every other week – three steps of uncovered terracing all around the pitch with a 100-seat stand along one side.

I'll never forget my time at Dulwich, and God knows I've tried. Our last fourteen games of the season produced two draws and twelve defeats. I conceded thirty-nine goals. The highlights included a 6-3 home defeat by Hendon and a 7-0 massacre at Basingstoke. I used to sneak into training at Palace and pray that none of the lads had seen the Dulwich score.

'How did it go on Saturday, Jim?'

'Great!'

'What was the score?'

'7–0.'

'Fantastic!'

The most valuable lesson of my four months at Dulwich was discovering that players love nothing more than deflecting blame. That's a skill I soon picked up; you need it to survive. One of Dulwich's centre-backs could have lazed for England. He gave me dodgy back-passes and left balls for me that should have been his. When opponents nipped in to score, he'd shake his head and point at me. I'd stand my ground without being too lippy. You didn't really know who you were dealing with. My caution was vindicated when I discovered that a couple of the Dulwich boys had spent time in prison for violent crime. I became quite edgy when anyone complained about teammates 'stabbing them in the back'.

When Dulwich finished the season rock bottom I felt more embarrassed than heartbroken. Nothing could have weakened my enthusiasm for football. I was a rising star at Crystal Palace with bigger and better things to look forward to. I was the man, I was the geezer, I told myself, as Mum drove me away in her battered old Vauxhall Carlton.

Two

GROWING PAINS

After leaving Dulwich, the next game I had an involvement in was Palace's first-ever match at Wembley, the 1990 FA Cup final against Manchester United. It was a massive day for the club. All the apprentices were there in our cup final blazers. I helped to supervise the VIP parking. At one point I saw a Mercedes arrive. The driver's door opened and closed but I didn't see anyone get out. Then Ronnie Corbett appeared.

Ian Wright wasn't fully fit for the final. He came on as a substitute with 20 minutes left and scored twice to earn a 3-3 draw. The game would be replayed four days later. We had a post-match party at Kensington Gardens Hotel, where I got pissed and tried to chat up various players' wives. I remember staggering over to Steve Coppell and yelling, 'All right, boss! What are you doing here?'

'What am *I* doing here? You're the one who's sixteen!'

We lost the replay 1-0. For the 1990/91 season my YTS wage soared to £35 a week. I was still living at home, and the lads who were staying in digs had their rent paid, so we didn't need a lot of cash. Now that Andy Woodman was too old I finally made it into the youth team. We played in the South East Counties League against the youth teams of other London clubs. The physical aspect of the game was easier because Dulwich had toughened me up. Many of the youth-team lads also played for Palace reserves in the Capital League. It was a good stepping stone. Back in the youth league they were like men against boys.

Overseas tournaments were a perk of playing in the youth team. Alan Smith was good at getting us trips abroad. Ron Noades and his wife came with us to Italy, where one of our players slipped a condom under their door. I played in a youth tournament in France. I've always been a strong kicker and I could launch the ball 100 yards. You could hear a collective gasp as the crowd craned their necks to see it disappear into orbit: 'Ahh! Ze Eeenglish are here!'

That season I also played two games for Carshalton in the Vauxhall-Opel Premier League, the same division Dulwich had been in. Their goalkeeper was banned at the time. He had been getting some stick from a fan, so he'd jumped into the crowd and chinned him. Later in the season, Alan Smith was promoted to become Palace's assistant manager, and Stuart Scott and Dave Garland took charge of the youth team. Stuart had been Alan Smith's assistant. Dave was a plumber who ran a team in the Southern Youth League.

By then I was finally getting some goalkeeper coaching. Nigel Martyn, Andy Woodman and myself trained one day a week with Peter Bonetti, the former Chelsea and England 'keeper. He taught us how to strengthen our legs to get more power when we took off to dive and showed us how to plant our feet to change direction quickly. I came on leaps and bounds. After six months of tuition I arrived one day to find that Peter wasn't there. We never saw him again, and we never found out why. He was working at a lot of clubs and we heard rumours that Palace didn't want him leaking any of their secrets. I could imagine the boardroom conversation:

'What if he tells them we had tuna for lunch yesterday?'

'Do you think he'd mention the new tiles in the dressing room?'

Peter Hucker, a former Queens Park Rangers goalkeeper, took over from Peter. But after a few weeks he disappeared too. My coaching at Crystal Palace went with him. I was there for another five years.

The youth team finished third in the league. I was playing well and getting good reports in the local papers, 'A Touch of Glass' being the first of many side-splitting puns on my name. In April 1991, with my YTS apprenticeship nearly over, Alan Smith offered me a two-year professional contract. There was no negotiation. He came up to me at the training ground and said, 'Two hundred quid a week'. I only got that much because of another lad in my year, Dean Gordon. He was an England Under-18 player and he wanted £200. He got it, so they gave it to me as well. I signed the contract in July, a month before my eighteenth birthday. Only three of the seven apprentices in my year were kept on. The third was Paul Brazier, a forward who was given a one-year deal. Of thirty schoolboys who had been on the first rung of

Steve Coppell's ladder two years earlier, twenty-seven had already been pushed off.

Palace's first team also finished third in their league, ten points ahead of Manchester United. Only Arsenal and Liverpool were above Crystal Palace; 1990/91 was the best season in their eighty-six-year history. Although Palace were never a massive club they could make their presence felt in the days when money wasn't the only factor behind a successful team. But football was changing. Before long, clubs like Palace would find it impossible to compete with their supposed superiors.

When I came back for pre-season training, my new home was the reserve-team dressing room. Just one more move up the corridor and I'd be in with the first team. Even though I was now a professional, I still played in the youth team because my August birthday made me eligible. I enjoyed my status as the oldest, and one of the most experienced, in the team. The transition from apprentice to professional was harder off the pitch than on it. The pros all had their cliques and I never really fitted in with any of them. Maybe it was a goalkeeper's mentality, the feeling that no one else can understand your situation. Whatever it was, a lot of my time was spent with the apprentices. I'd go into their dressing room, sit down, and act as if I was waiting for a bus. I loved making them laugh.

At least there were no more boots or toilets to clean, and I had an apprentice to take care of my kit. My first boot boy was Glen Little, a midfielder who went on to play for Burnley. Palace's penny-pinching was as frustrating as ever. If Glen missed his bus, by the time he arrived my kit would have been nicked by another player's apprentice. Glen would have to scamper around looking for various rejects. But life was a lot easier. I didn't turn up until ten o'clock and I was away three hours later. I was still living with my parents at Worcester Park and Dad would come home from an early shift to find I'd already gone back to bed. He'd lecture me about making the most of my time, saying I should be studying or doing extra training, but no footballer I knew bothered with anything like that.

The first team were still on a high after their third-place finish. Ian Wright couldn't stop scoring goals, although it didn't do a lot for his personality. Wrighty could be very unpleasant. Maybe he had a chip on his shoulder because he came late to the professional game. He had been twenty-one and working as a plasterer when he joined Palace from Greenwich Borough in 1985. In some ways, though, his 'fuck you' attitude made him a great player. He once kicked me in the face during a training session. Steve Coppell bollocked him, but I accepted it as an occupational hazard. Neither Wrighty nor me suffered fools gladly. If someone had a dig at me I had a dig back. The older players hated that. It looked like a lack of respect, but it wasn't. Once you start taking the blame as a goalkeeper, you're finished. You need to be strong-willed because the team's fate is on your shoulders.

One day when I was training with the first team a friend of Ian's called Tony Finnigan was on my side. I went to pick the ball up but Tony whipped it out of my hands.

'What are you doing, Tone?' I said.

Wrighty came over, shouting and swearing: 'Don't talk to him like that!'

'Fuck off!'

'That's it! I want you round the back now!'

He eventually calmed down, but we never spoke again and he left Palace soon after. Our argument marred my memory of someone I should have good memories about. I've seen Wrighty a couple of times since but he blanked me. If we meet again I'll give him back one of the boots he wore in that 1990 FA Cup final. A year after the final I went to see one of my youth-team colleagues who had been Wrighty's boot boy but was released after his YTS. He'd nicked the left boot, and he gave it to me.

Some players were more helpful to youngsters than Ian Wright. I've come across very few goalkeepers, for instance, who haven't been willing to pass on advice. If we start stitching each other up we've got no one. Gary O'Reilly, a midfielder, was also very encouraging. One afternoon Dave Garland asked him to work with the youth-team defenders, so Gary helped them with heading and passing. There isn't enough of that in football. Clubs rarely make the experienced professionals work with their youth-team counterparts. Maybe it's seen as competition. At football clubs you often hear phrases like 'You've got to look after yourself in this game because no one else will'. This attitude is often justified by 'survival of the fittest'. That's fine for players like Ian Wright who have superhuman motivation; it's not so good for the majority – young lads away from home for the first time, or from broken homes. They need guidance, on and off the pitch, but they rarely get it.

In the summer of 1991, Crystal Palace were ideally placed to become a real force in English football. Then it all went wrong, in a way no one could have predicted. Ron Noades was interviewed on a television documentary about football and race. He said:

The black players at this club lend the side a lot of skill and flair, but you also need white players in there to balance things up and give the team some brains and some common sense. When you are getting into mid-winter in England, you need a few of the maybe hard white men to carry the artistic black players through.

These comments made headlines for weeks. I don't think anyone but Ron will ever know why he made them. Football is one of the most colour-blind professions in Britain. Black and white players treat each other the same. Any differences are cultural. In my experience, when black players go out they tend to dress immaculately and drink spirits, while white players throw lager down their throats until they can't stand. On the pitch, football mirrors life. Some people work hard and some don't, but it's not a case of black and white.

Around half the squad at Palace was black. In Ian Wright, Mark Bright, John Salako and Andy Gray, some of the team's most important players were black. By questioning their work rate, and even their intelligence, Ron Noades arguably ended the most successful period in Palace's history. Ian Wright reported his chairman to the Commission for Racial Equality and demanded a transfer. But although Wrighty was justifiably angry, there was some suggestion that he also saw Noades' comments as an excuse to get away from Palace. His goals had attracted the attention of bigger clubs, and now he could leave without being accused of disloyalty. He joined Arsenal and went on to become their all-time record goalscorer. For Palace, it was all downhill from there.

A few weeks after my run-in with Wrighty I was training with the youth team. Most of the time I was the only goalkeeper there and every morning I faced an hour of shooting sessions under constant rapid fire. We trained with balls the first team were finished with because they were knackered. They had to be pumped up incredibly hard to keep their shape. It was like playing with rocks. I saw a shot come out of the sun and put up my right hand to stop it. This bullet of a ball bent my hand back, causing a sharp pain. I went to see one of the physios, David West. He examined my wrist and said it might be a fractured scaphoid. That didn't mean a thing to me. He sent me to a hospital in New Malden where the club had a consultant, but the consultant didn't see me. A nurse took an X-ray and told me to come back in two weeks. I trained as a striker for a fortnight, and when I went back another nurse took another X-ray. They thought it was a sprained tendon which would heal itself, so I was told to carry on as normal.

Three months later I was training with the first team when striker David White hit a shot which I blocked with my left hand. The hand bent back and there was a sharp pain in my wrist. Back at the hospital there was still no sign of a consultant. A nurse took yet another X-ray but couldn't spot anything. This time I didn't go back for the second X-ray, thinking it was another sprain. Every morning David West or the other physio, a Norwegian called Toré, had me plunge my hands in a bucket of ice then stretch them against a wall. They'd strap the hands forward so they wouldn't bend back so far when a ball hit them. It was agony. I was taking painkillers like they were Smarties. I trained and played like that for the last four months of the 1991/92 season, but I did well and the youth team won the South East Counties League.

The FA Youth Cup brought more success. The tournament works on the same principle as the FA Cup: every youth team in the country enters, from non-League upwards. Palace beat Charlton and Chelsea then faced Wimbledon in a two-legged semi-final. We won the first leg and drew the second to reach the final. We were ecstatic in the dressing room afterwards, until Steve Coppell said, in his inimitable style, 'Make the most of the good times, boys, because the bad times are just around the corner.'

'Right... thanks, boss.'

Reaching the final was even sweeter because of the opposition – Manchester United. This final has gone into football folklore as the point at which 'Fergie's Fledglings' emerged. Even then everyone knew that David Beckham, Ryan Giggs, Paul Scholes, Nicky Butt and the Neville brothers had the potential to dominate the English game for years. The first leg of the final was at Selhurst Park at the end of April in front of 8,000 people, the biggest crowd of my career at that point. Butt gave United the lead and Beckham lashed an unstoppable twenty-yard drive into the top corner of my goal. We were trailing 2-1 when Ben Thornley scored a third for United in the last minute. The second leg was at Old Trafford the following Wednesday.

However, before that, on the Saturday after the first leg, the first team were to play their last match of the season, at Queens Park Rangers. Thanks to Steve Coppell the team had survived the loss of Ian Wright and the uproar over Ron Noades's comments to finish mid-table. Then, the day before the QPR game, Nigel Martyn got injured. It was amazing: Nigel was *never* injured. His deputy, Andy Woodman, was injured as well. This was the chance I'd dreamed of. I waited for the phone call. It never came.

The next day I discovered that Palace had signed Neil Sullivan on a month's loan from Wimbledon, to play one match. Alan Smith had been left in charge by Steve Coppell. Alan must have been desperate to avoid playing me. He had to get permission from the Football Association to sign Sullivan because the transfer deadline had passed. Alan told the FA that I was injured, even though I'd played four games that week – for the youth team and the reserves, and a testimonial. I don't know why he did it. That summed up the club's lack of youth development. For the first time in my life I felt disillusioned with foot-ball. I would have felt even worse if I'd known my career would soon be hanging in the balance.

After missing out on my League debut, Manchester United at Old Trafford was a decent consolation. Ryan Giggs had sat out the first leg of the Youth Cup final but he played that night. He was already a regular in United's first team. Palace shocked the 16,000 crowd by scoring in the first minute to go 3-2 down on aggregate. We had chances to equalise but didn't take them. Just before half-time United's Ben Thornley scored to make it 4-2. Early in the second half Simon Davies smashed in a close-range shot: 5-2. I got a hand to it, and after the match I discovered it had broken my little finger. It hurt like hell but I wasn't going to come off early at Old Trafford. There was no substitute 'keeper on the bench anyway back then. The only way an injured goalie left the pitch was in a body bag. United scored again before we pulled one back: 6–3 on aggregate. It was disappointing to lose but great to have got there.

There are many reasons for the contrasting fortunes of Crystal Palace and Manchester United since that night in 1992. Here's one: at the time of writing, eight of United's eleven players from the FA Youth Cup final second leg are still in professional football; most of them formed the nucleus of the 1999 Treble-winning team. Of the Palace side who started the same match, only one is still playing profession-ally: George Ndah at Wolves. In fact, a few weeks after the final, seven of the Palace team were released. Within a year, nine were out of foot-ball. Manchester United had the foresight to keep their youngsters and develop them; Palace never thought past the following Saturday. Some players were so disheartened that they stopped playing at eighteen, others drifted into non-League. And if coaching in the professional game wasn't up to scratch, non-League was even worse.

At the end of the season Alan Smith called me in to his office. I had a year left on my contract but I'd been playing well and the club wanted me to sign a year's extension for another £100 a week, bring-ing my wage to £300. I wanted to tackle Alan about his signing of Neil Sullivan, but I didn't have the courage. Maybe I didn't want to risk hearing him say that I wasn't good enough to play for the first team. I kept my mouth shut and signed the extension. Paul Brazier was released. Twenty-eight down, two to go.

The new deal at Palace didn't mean I wasn't open to other offers of work. That summer, Dad said, 'Do you fancy working at Wimbledon?' He knew the bloke who ran the security company. Now, I've always loved tennis. I like the fact that the result is down to you, whereas in football you're at the mercy of so many others. I was selected as a player escort, with a gold sash on my arm to prove it. The other escorts were students, glad of £700 for a fortnight. It was good money to me as well, more than I was earning at Palace, but my main motivation was the chance to meet the players, Gabriela Sabatini in particular. She was the number one tennis babe at the time and I had admired her from afar for years.

During the championships I found myself with the privilege of guarding Gabriela. When she was on court I stood behind her chair;

whenever she needed taking anywhere I was happy to volunteer. I even walked her home one night. I escorted her to the gates and some people started following her. She was worried they might be a bit dodgy so she asked me to walk her back to the house where she was staying. If she'd known some of the thoughts I'd had about her during the previous few years she'd have run to them for help. At the time I thought she was being melodramatic, but a year later Monica Seles was stabbed at a tournament in Germany.

Walking Gabriela Sabatini home was a once-in-a-lifetime opportunity. I tried desperately to find some common ground between us. My opening gambit was a corker which still fills me with pride today.

'Do you like football?'

'Yes,' she replied. 'I like football. I am a River Plate fan.'

I tried to explain that I was a footballer and I played for Crystal Palace, but it didn't seem to impress her all that much. Either that or she couldn't speak very good English. I like to think it was the latter.

When we got to her door I was too scared to try and take it any further. However, I'm under no illusions about whether or not she would have invited me in. A lanky eighteen-year-old in a hat that was too small and a jacket that was too big was never really going to race her motor. I looked like I worked for the gas board.

I walked Boris Becker to and from court a few times, or rather he walked me – he didn't really need escorting. It was the year Andre Agassi won the tournament, and for his second-round match I walked him to and from Court Two and stood behind his chair. I also stood guard on the final day when he came outside with the trophy. Tennis players are superb athletes. They are incredibly focused, even on the practice courts. The contrast between them and the sportsmen I worked with on a daily basis during the football season was staggering.

I met lots of other famous players, including Fred Perry and Chris Evert. Chris was standing outside the dressing rooms with a pen and pad. I asked her if she wanted my autograph. She gave me a bored look and said 'No'. Taxi for Glass.

Some players I'd never heard of wanted to be escorted. Maybe they thought they were important, or they wanted to feel important. Maybe they just wanted someone to talk to. To me, the likes of Gabriela Sabatini were superstars, but I soon realised that they were just ordinary people with an extraordinary ability. I should have known that already, having grown up with people like Ian Wright. At the start of the tournament I was star-struck; by the end I understood it more.

My life has been peppered with experiences where I find myself in a totally different world to the one I'm used to. I don't know if it's luck or because I put myself in those positions. Back in pre-season training I couldn't wait to tell the lads.

'Guess what? I walked Gabriela Sabatini home the other night!'

'Yeah, all right, Jim.'

I once ran up the pitch in the last minute and saved a football club. Honest.

Three

THE RAGGY DOLLS

Crystal Palace had finished the 1991/92 season as a mid-table First Division side. We started 1992/93 in the Premier League. When Sky television was launched in the early 1990s, they decided that football was the key to success. The Football Association had a deal with ITV which paid First Division clubs a total of £11 million a year. Teams in the Second, Third and Fourth Divisions received less, but the gap wasn't huge.

When the ITV contract ran out in 1992, Sky stepped forward. They offered the top-flight clubs £61 million a year for five years, on condition that the First Division split from the rest of the Football League and became the Premier League. The 'product', as the sport would soon become known, was repackaged and live matches were made available only to satellite viewers.

Many First Division chairmen had been complaining that the League's smaller clubs were getting too much television revenue. These chairmen were all in favour of the Sky deal and the FA couldn't sign the contract quickly enough. They believed that making rich clubs richer was better than trying to strengthen the game's roots.

After 104 years as a united body, the Football League was split. Those at the top were handed the money to stay there. The rest were left to get by on a few crumbs. Overnight, the gap between rich and poor grew wider than ever. Trying to bridge this gulf would bring dozens of clubs to the brink of bankruptcy.

At first, the Premier League was just a name. The only changes were surface details, such as referees wearing green shirts instead of black. But behind the scenes more than £300 million was about to flood into football. Here was an opportunity for massive investment in facilities and the development of young players. Would the clubs take it?

★

During pre-season training I caught the first ball that was kicked at me and a terrible pain ran through both wrists. I went to David West and this time demanded to see a consultant. David sent me to a hand specialist who took two X-rays and put them on the board. The scaphoid bone in each wrist had broken in half.

The fractures had started as hairline cracks. If my wrists had been examined straight away they would have been put in plaster and the cracks would have healed, but because they were left to be battered every day by knackered old footballs, there were now holes between the bones. My only chance of a football career was an operation. The success rate was fifty-fifty, but it was no gamble. Without the operation I was finished.

The specialist put me under general anaesthetic and chiselled out a segment of bone from my right hip. He opened the back of my wrists, crushed the scaphoid bones up, then put my hip bone in the holes and pinned them together. It would take ten months to discover if the operations had worked. I was angry at Palace's physios and the consultant who hadn't been there when I needed him. Nigel Martyn would have been looked at, but I was just a kid. David West said there wasn't much point in me turning up every day. I went in a couple of times a week to jog, with my wrists in plaster casts. My colleagues were very sympathetic: 'Hey, Jim! We told you what would happen if you didn't stop wanking!'

When the casts came off I sometimes trained up front with my hands in plastic guards. My wrists were X-rayed every two months, and every two months there were cracks. The first six months were like a holiday. I could lie in in the mornings and have a few beers with my mates on Friday night. I went on holiday to Sussex with Mum, Dad and Iain. We must have been a real sight at mealtimes as Mum had to cut up my food as well as Iain's.

Ten months after the operation there was still no sign of progress. The surgeon referred me to a specialist in bones that don't heal. He examined my wrists, said the only option was to operate again, and warned me I was likely to get arthritis in later life because my bones had been so badly damaged. The day before the operation I twisted my ankle in training, so I staggered into hospital on crutches. The specialist took a chunk of bone from my other hip. When he opened the left wrist he found it had healed, so he removed the pin and closed it. He had to do the right one again. I was in hospital for five days so when I came out at least my ankle had healed. For the next few weeks I slept with battery-powered machines strapped to my hands which sent an electric pulse through my wrists. Now I had to play the waiting game again.

The fallout from Ron Noades's comments about black players continued to haunt Palace throughout 1992/93. At the start of the season Mark Bright had joined Sheffield Wednesday. If anyone objected to Noades's words it was Mark. He was replaced by Paul Williams in a swap deal which also saw us receive £375,000. This was not Palace's greatest piece of business. Paul Williams scored only one goal all season – and that was against Palace before he moved to the club.

We struggled before Christmas without Wright or Bright but found some form in the new year. In the final week of the season Palace were nine points clear of Oldham, who occupied the third and final relegation place. Then Oldham won their two games in hand. Going into the last day of the season Palace could still be relegated if they lost and Oldham won – and that's exactly what happened. We went down on goal difference with 49 points, the highest-ever total for a relegated club. Just two years after finishing third, the loss of the Wright-Bright strike force had proved decisive. During the summer, Steve Coppell left Palace by mutual consent after nine years. His departure was the shape of things to come in football. Losing top-flight status in 1993 was a bigger blow than ever thanks to the now huge difference in television revenue between the Premier League and Division One. With the stakes so high, chairmen became increasingly impatient if their Premier League place was threatened.

Coppell was replaced by his former assistant, Alan Smith. Alan had been an excellent youth-team manager, bringing through future international players such as Gareth Southgate and John Salako. Ron Noades wanted someone who would toe the line and Alan fitted the bill. He was in football for the love of the game; he certainly didn't need the money. Alan had played professionally but a car crash ended his career. He moved into property development and was a wealthy man when he joined Palace as a part-time youth coach. When Ron Noades persuaded him to go full time it actually cost Alan money.

Alan had learned a lot from our youth-team trips to Italy and France. He was very methodical. He encouraged us to eat pasta instead of chips and to spend time stretching. From my first year at Palace, the start of every season saw great emphasis on the wonders of stretching. Before training, the physio would take us through a twenty-minute session which warmed and loosened every muscle. Then, one day, the physio was busy and the stretching lasted ten minutes. Then five. Then he couldn't make it and a coach would tell us to jog around the pitch before going straight into a game. Good intentions never lasted.

One of Alan's first moves as manager was to introduce club blazers. Until then, the top players had turned up in expensive suits and the other lads had looked scruffy in comparison. You could see a divide in the squad and Alan was right to create a more united image. He brought in David Kemp, a former Carlisle and Plymouth forward, as his assistant.

I was banging in goals during training while I waited for my right wrist to heal; David thought I was a striker until someone told him otherwise. I once nutmegged Gareth Southgate and slid the ball past Nigel Martyn into the goal. But Alan Smith didn't like me training up front: 'I've got millions of pounds of talent here, and *you* want to get involved?' You never really knew where you stood with Alan. Most of the time he was very quiet and calm. Next thing he'd be chucking teacups across the dressing room and calling everyone a wanker. But he had some novel ways of brightening up training sessions. When he wanted someone to whip in a cross with a bit of pace on it, he'd yell, 'Violence!' Another of his catchphrases was 'Fuck my granny!' for those moments when 'Oh, I say!' just doesn't seem enough.

Ten months after my second operation the specialist announced that my right wrist had healed. He said I was ready to be a goalkeeper again. But both wrists were very weak. I'd lost a lot of movement and they could only bend back so far. The thought of balls thudding into my hands frightened me. Twenty minutes into my first day of goal-keeper training for nearly two years, I broke my finger. I went down at winger Stuart Massey's feet and he stamped on my hand. It was a blessing in disguise; it gave me six weeks to do a lot more work on my wrists, and at the end of the 1993/94 season I came back flying. I played some reserve games and did well. Palace were to return to the Premier League at the first attempt, having gathered 90 points from 46 games and having kept most of the previous season's squad. My contract was almost up, so Alan Smith called me in to his office.

'We're letting Andy Woodman go,' he said. 'You're going to be Nigel Martyn's number two.'

This was fantastic news. I signed a one-year contract for £300 a week. And no, that sentence is not missing any noughts: in 1994, a Premier League goalkeeper signed a contract for £300 a week.

If you come through the ranks with a club it can be hard to get a decent deal. You might think clubs would look after their own, but actually they tend to take you for granted. Even players who arrive from non-League are offered more. That's why so many people leave the club they started at. But money wasn't my motivation. I was excited at the thought of going to places like Old Trafford and Anfield, if only on the substitutes bench.

We went to Portugal for a pre-season tour, to the same place we'd gone to five years earlier when I'd just signed my YTS forms. Nigel Martyn couldn't go because he was having a hernia operation, so I was due to play every match. Ray Wilkins, the former Manchester United and England midfielder, had joined Palace as a player/coach. In a training session I went to tackle him but he sent me the wrong way and my left knee locked. I'd torn my cartilage. We had no crutches and I couldn't get a flight home for two days. I was hopping around thinking, 'Great, another thing to tell my parents'. Just when things seemed to be going right, it all fell apart again.

Back home I had another operation. The surgeon accidentally cut through the part of the knee which produces fluid, so every time I tried to play my knee swelled up. Palace needed a number two 'keeper so they signed Rhys Wilmot from Torquay. When I got fit after four months there was no room for me. Rhys and Nigel trained with the first team; I trained with the reserves, and shared the reserve matches with Rhys. One game a fortnight is not ideal for a twenty-one-year-old footballer's development.

Training was the same as in my youth-team days – lots of running and five-a-sides. My only specialist coaching was from the kit man. Vic Bertinelli played in goal for a Sunday team and fancied himself as a coach. His heart was in the right place, and Vic has gone on to be an excellent 'keeper coach, but at the time he was naïve. I had to run into the middle of the goal and spin around three times before someone hit a shot at me. I'd just come back from a career-threatening injury, and he had me getting dizzy then blocking shots with the same rock-hard balls that had caused the injuries.

Ex-Palace 'keeper Perry Suckling also had scaphoid problems which may have been linked to these balls. Whenever Toré the physio found one he stabbed it with scissors so it couldn't be used any more. I mentioned the training balls to Steve Kember, the reserve-team coach. His response was, 'Stop moaning and just get on with it!' I called him a has-been.

'I may be a has-been but at least I'm not a never-will-be!'

Matches were fine because you've always got a decent ball, but it was hard to train when I knew the balls could smash my wrists to pieces. It's hard to punch a ball when you're thinking, 'If this goes wrong, my career's over.' It was physically difficult to punch with one hand anyway because I'd lost so much strength in my wrists. That's why I tried to catch everything for the rest of my career, sometimes against my better judgement.

Before my injuries I'd been regarded as a bright young thing – either a star of the youth team or a precocious member of first-team training sessions. Not any more. The reserves were known as 'the raggy dolls' – the ones nobody wanted. A lot of the reserve squad weren't regarded as potential first-teamers, except in times of dire emergency, and I was surplus to requirements. The reserves had to attend every first-team home match and were fined if they didn't. Those players who were feeling bitter or rebellious turned up one minute before kick-off and cleared off as soon as the final whistle sounded. It was a dispiriting existence.

An unexpected highlight was a trip to Hong Kong to play their national champions. Our hosts were expecting Crystal Palace's Premier League stars. They got the raggy dolls instead. There was £10,000 prize money for the winning team, but Alan Smith made the mistake of telling us that if we won the money would go into the players' pool. This meant the first team would take a cut. Suitably inspired, we flew out on Friday morning, arrived Saturday night local time, and went straight out on the piss. On Sunday we nursed our hangovers in the national stadium and lost on penalties.

I came back to more of the same as a raggy doll, feeling that I would never pull on a first-team Palace jersey. My problems were put into perspective when my little brother Iain became very ill. I was pretty cut up about it and I visited him in hospital every day. Iain made a slow recovery. Ray Wilkins was the only person at Palace who ever asked how he was. I shouldn't have been surprised. We're blokes. We don't talk about the important stuff.

On the evening of Wednesday 25 January 1995, I drove to Selhurst Park with Dad. Palace were playing Manchester United. There was always a great atmosphere when United were in town and the stakes were high for both sides. United were second in the table; Palace were just above the relegation zone. In the second half, Eric Cantona kicked out at Palace's Richard Shaw. The referee booked the Frenchman for the second time and sent him off. I was sitting six rows back from the touchline when he prowled past en route to the dressing room. Because it was Cantona, all eyes were on him. Lots of Palace fans were booing and taunting him. The raggy dolls were trying to look cool. I saw someone run past me down towards the side of the pitch. He began screaming at Cantona. The United star put his hand on the advertising hoarding and in one fluid movement he vaulted it and planted his studs in the man's chest.

'Shit!'

Cantona was immediately surrounded by police and stewards while the crowd went berserk.

On the radio on the way home, the man he attacked was revealed as a Palace fan called Matthew Simmons. Simmons said he'd been strolling along, minding his own business, when Cantona walked past. Perhaps struggling to recall his exact words, Simmons claimed he'd said, 'It's an early shower for you, Cantona!'

This was the world I'd spent most of my life trying to enter. A fortnight later I made it.

Four

JUST LOOKING

Alan Smith rang me on a Thursday night in February. 'Get yourself to Fratton Park tomorrow morning,' he said. 'You're playing for Portsmouth on Saturday.' Portsmouth were struggling in Division One. I drove down and met the manager, former England defender Terry Fenwick. His goalkeeper, Alan Knight, had been sent off a couple of weeks earlier, so Portsmouth needed a 'keeper on loan to play against Millwall while he was suspended. I stayed in a hotel on the Friday night and woke up feeling sick with nerves for the first time in my life. The pouring rain matched my mood. But nothing could stop me now. After so many years and disappointments, this was it. Three years after Neil Sullivan had taken my place for Palace's last game of the season, after two broken wrists, two broken fingers and a torn cartilage, my Football League debut was here at last. 11 February 1995 was a date I would never forget.

I arrived at Fratton Park. The pitch was waterlogged. The game was off.

My debut actually came a week later at Roker Park, Sunderland, in front of 14,000 people. It was a big match. Sunderland were in the Division One relegation zone; Portsmouth were two places higher. I was very nervous again, almost to the point of vomiting. This was my first game of first-team football since Carshalton four years earlier. Before kick-off we changed ends. As I ran towards the home supporters, thousands of them applauded me. 'That's nice!' I thought, and raised my hands to return their warm wishes. Thousands of Sunderland fans screamed, 'ARRRGH!'

We drew 2-2 and I played quite well. After the game I realised that my parents had driven up, which is typical of the support they have always given me. Alan Knight returned from suspension and played

Portsmouth's next seven matches. I signed for another month on loan and sat on the bench. Then Terry Fenwick committed heresy – he dropped Alan Knight. Alan was a Portsmouth legend. It was the first time he had been dropped in years. Terry was looking to bring through a younger 'keeper so he played me at Port Vale. We lost 1–0. I did well on a wet night but made a mistake for the goal. I'd still done enough to impress Terry so I played the next match against Bolton. It was my first home game, for anyone. On my way to the home end I applauded the fans and thanked God I would receive a warmer reception than Sunderland's supporters had given me. Here we go...

'Fuck off, Glass! You're not wanted! FUCK OFF!'

One or two Portsmouth fans were a little unhappy that Alan Knight had been dropped. But I performed quite well in a 1–1 draw and was due to play against Tranmere the following Saturday. Then, during the week, I picked up a chest infection. I was prone to those throughout my career – the legacy of too many winters spent standing around on frozen football pitches. While I shivered in bed, Alan Knight was back in goal. A few days later I watched Palace on television against Manchester United in an FA Cup semi-final. The match finished 2–2. Nigel Martyn broke his finger and was ruled out for a month. Rhys Wilmot would play in goal for the replay; I would be on the bench. My Palace contract was due to run out at the end of the season, and before I left Portsmouth Terry Fenwick asked me not to sign a new one. He wanted me at Fratton Park next season with a good chance of first-team football.

The semi-final replay was at Villa Park. During my warm-up I threw myself all over the place to try and feel part of the occasion. As everyone else was walking out for the game, I staggered in, covered in mud. The most memorable incident of the match was Roy Keane's stamp on Gareth Southgate, which earned Keane a red card. I turned to the linesman.

'Linesman! You must have seen that!'

Andy Cole was in the Manchester United dugout a few yards to my right, cup-tied after his recent £7 million transfer from Newcastle. He leaned over to me in his trenchcoat and beret, just like Frank Spencer, and said, 'Why don't you shut your fucking mouth?'

I searched hard for the right response.

'Why don't you fuck off? You big-time twat!'

He squared up to me. Alex Ferguson stepped between us. Palace defender Chris Coleman put his arm around me and dragged me back. 'I understand, son,' he said, 'but there's 10,000 United fans ready to throttle you.' I turned around and they were screaming abuse at me.

'Right... I'll shut up now.'

United won 2-0. After the game Andy Cole was standing outside the players' bar. He started again: 'Do you want some? What are you giving it?' We had a little slanging match, then I went for a drink.

I hadn't spent much time with the first team and everyone was in their cliques or with their families. The place was crawling with United players too. Andy Cole and Paul Ince were staring at me. 'Sod this,' I thought, 'I'm off.'

On the bus back to London the lads were laughing about my encounter with the superstars. John Humphrey, our right-back, said, 'Jim, you should have just said to Andy Cole, "Listen, pal. What have you ever done?"'

A similar thing happened with Glenn Hoddle. Palace played a reserve-team friendly at Chelsea when Hoddle was their manager. We sent a load of kids and trialists and won 4-0. Being a Tottenham fan, Glenn Hoddle was a legend to me. All through the game I was think-ing how great it was to be on the same pitch as him. Right at the end Chelsea got a free-kick just outside the penalty area. Hoddle went to whip in a quick one while I was lining up my wall. I read it, scampered along my line and caught it, then shouted, 'All right, Glenn?' He yelled, 'How many League games have you played, you cheeky little twat?' After the final whistle I thought I'd better apologise. Not that I'd done anything wrong, but this was Glenn Hoddle. I shook his hand.

'Sorry, Glenn. I didn't mean any disrespect.'

'Yeah. You were a bit out of line there, son.'

Not 'Oh, don't worry about it'. I thought, 'You absolute prat'. My opinion didn't change a few years later when Hoddle declared that disabled people were paying for their sins in a former life. It was hard to believe anyone could think that, especially someone who had reached his position. I was embarrassed to remember that Hoddle used to be my hero.

After the FA Cup semi-final replay Rhys Wilmot continued to deputise for Nigel Martyn and I spent the next three Premier League matches on the bench, at home to Spurs and away at QPR and Blackburn. Palace, the definitive yo-yo team, were relegated after just one season back in the Premier League. Ron Noades and Alan Smith had a huge row about who was to blame and Alan jumped ship before he could be pushed. Noades appointed Ray Lewington and Peter Nicholas as joint managers. Lewey had been first-team coach and Peter was youth-team manager. Noades made himself director of football, with responsibility for signing players. He was fed up with managers making bad signings, as he saw them, so he would show people how it should be done. One of his buys was a striker called Gareth Taylor. Noades paid Bristol Rovers £750,000 for Taylor and gave him a massive salary. Taylor turned out to be stunningly mediocre. He scored only two goals before Noades let him go after five months just to get him off the wage bill. Nice to see the Sky television money being put to good use.

My contract was about to run out and Terry Fenwick hadn't been in touch. Ron Noades called me in to his office. 'Sign for another year,' he said. 'We're going to offload Rhys Wilmot and you'll play all the reserve games. If you're not happy at any time, come and tell me. I'll tear up your contract and you can leave on a free transfer.'

I didn't know what to do, so I spoke to Ray Lewington and told him I needed to play some football. He said, 'Stay and I'll get you another ten grand.' I had to get something sorted so I signed a one-year contract for £500 a week. Two days later Terry Fenwick rang to say he wanted me at Portsmouth.

At least I finally got a taste of first-team action at the end of the season, if only in a five-a-side competition. The *Evening Standard* tournament was held every year for clubs in the London area and televised across the UK. It was my first time on television – and I marked it by scoring a goal. Our game against Wycombe went to a penalty shoot-out. The Wycombe 'keeper and me both saved our first four, then he scored against me and I smashed the ball past him. Penalties started again and Wycombe eventually won. Those tournaments were great fun for players and fans. All the big names played. Teams like Leyton Orient and Brentford had their day against Arsenal and Spurs. There was nothing at stake except enjoying a game of football. The tournament was scrapped the following year, because enjoying a game of football doesn't get you another million in the bank.

★

In July 1995, with Palace back in Division One, I turned up for pre-season training. To my amazement, Rhys Wilmot was still there. During the summer Ray Lewington and Peter Nicholas had decided they wanted three goalkeepers. I was back to square one. Rhys and Nigel trained with the first team as before while I developed as a goalkeeper by playing five-a-sides with the reserves. My time at Portsmouth had whetted my appetite for League football but Palace were making no attempt to push me into the first-team squad. It never occurred to anyone to even put me on the bench now and then. All that mattered was whoever was number one at the time.

Sometimes I played up front for a friend's team on Sundays, just to get a game and enjoy it. My mates could never understand why a professional footballer was so keen to turn up for a Sunday-morning kickabout. I had to play under someone else's name because Palace wouldn't have liked it. They could have argued I was being unprofessional. To me, it just showed how much I loved football. In one match the score was 1-1 when I came on as a substitute in the second half. I scored four goals in five minutes. The following week I saw the lad whose identity I'd borrowed. 'Cheers, Jim!' he said. 'You've done wonders for my goalscoring figures!'

At the end of the year I signed with my first agent. Les Sealey, a former Manchester United goalkeeper, approached me after a reserve game. He was looking for clients to join the Stellar Agency. I assumed he was on commission but I didn't like to ask. Stellar's office walls were covered in photographs of their clients, including the snooker player John Higgins and the West Indian cricketer Brian Lara. They even had Lara's bat from his record-breaking 375 Test innings. These days Stellar have most of the England football team on their books, but they were just starting out then. I joined Stellar on the understanding that they would get ten per cent of any signing-on fee – a payment players often receive when they sign a new contract. I'd never had a signing-on fee, which was one reason why I needed an agent.

Football was changing rapidly. Until the early 1990s European clubs were allowed to field only three foreign players. This rule was abolished under European Union employment laws. Meanwhile, Jean-Marc Bosman became a contender for the title of First Famous Belgian. Bosman was a midfielder with Belgian club Liege. His contract had ended in 1994. He wanted to join a French team but Liege didn't want him to go. Under Belgian football rules, they could keep Bosman's registration and stop him playing for anyone else. Bosman thought this amounted to restraint of trade. The European courts agreed, quite rightly. But the judge made a ruling that destroyed the traditional transfer system of every European country, including Britain, where the system was relatively fair and had worked well for decades.

If a player moved between British clubs after his contract had run out, his new club had to pay a transfer fee to his previous employer. This reflected the loss of that player to the club he had just left, as well as the efforts they'd made to develop him as a footballer. Smaller clubs made their money by selling their best players to teams from higher divisions. The Bosman ruling cut that lifeline. Now, any player aged over twenty-four can join another club when his contract finishes and his former club does not receive a penny.

Players at the bottom of the professional ladder always had the chance of a move to the top. That changed in the mid-1990s. The abolition of the three-foreigners rule meant any number of foreign players could come to Britain and expect first-team football. The Bosman ruling also meant that many of them could come on free transfers. Instead of paying £500,000 for a promising kid from the Second Division, clubs could pay a similar amount in wages over three years for a matured and proven foreign player.

No one who watches Thierry Henry or Ruud Van Nistelrooy can deny that foreign players have improved the Premiership. As well as bringing skill, they have also helped to instil a more professional attitude. Europeans are happy to have a glass of wine with a meal but will generally forego running around at three o'clock in the morning with a traffic cone on their head. However, there is a big difference between enhancing the game with the best foreign players and swamping it with also-rans simply because they're cheap.

My generation of English footballers was betrayed by the system. Instead of investing in the coaching and facilities which would help us fulfil our potential, the English game bought ready-made foreign talent. Clubs began importing anyone with three caps for Lithuania; young British players had to go to smaller clubs to get a game. Then they're in the small clubs' system of poor facilities, poor coaching and poor football.

One argument is that we Brits should have worked harder to make ourselves better than the imports. Fair enough, up to a point, but no amount of graft can make up for the damage done since childhood. Take a French player. Since the age of six he's been coached by professionals at his local club's academy. Then take an English player. He's been coached by someone's dad and told to 'Get rid of it!' whenever he's under any pressure.

From when I started playing for the cub scouts, the emphasis with all my teams was on league position. Team talks revolved around how far we were ahead of them or how many points we needed to catch them. But learning to control and pass the ball is far more important than finishing at the top of some local league. Children shouldn't even play competitive matches until they're eleven or twelve. They don't on the Continent. Why not call it a goal if a team puts ten passes together? In that game there are no positions, and kids can be encouraged to play everywhere before being put in the position that suits their game best. What happens instead is that coaches take a seven-year-old and say, 'He's tall, he'll make a central defender'. For the rest of their career they're labelled. They only develop the skill to do that job instead of being proficient in all departments.

Winning the World Cup in 1966 made us complacent. We didn't see the Europeans and South Americans coming up on our blind side, concentrating on technique and developing their youngsters to be complete footballers. We stuck with the same mentality: be hard, get pissed, run it off the next day. Manchester United were one of the few English clubs to invest in youth, and look how it paid off. Arsenal, Chelsea and the rest employed imports to fill the holes left by the English system's inadequacy. The Premiership is a bunch of stop-gaps. It's papering over the cracks of English football.

The failure to invest in youth can be seen whenever the England national team tries to justify its hype. Only a handful of English players are good enough for the world stage. Whoever is England manager won't change the fact that we don't have enough young players coming through. The next generation are inspired by the top foreign players they see in the Premier League. They copy these stars' names in the playground but they don't know how to copy their skills. So are English footballers genetically inferior to the French or Italians? Believing that is no better than believing Ron Noades's comments about black players.

We didn't need a huge influx of foreign players; we needed foreign coaches to bring the best out of our players. Foreign coaches have been the people trying the hardest to move English football forward, because they see that England is years behind the rest of Europe. These men are great in terms of the enlightenment they bring to the English game. The problem for the England team's prospects is that they bring in foreign players. They only have a year to produce or they're out. That isn't long enough to build a squad of homegrown talent so they bring in players they have worked with abroad.

By 1995 I'd started using the first-team dressing room instead of the reserves', not that I'd suddenly earned the right to be there. I'd spent years watching players come and go from the first-team area while I loitered down the corridor. I didn't care about the etiquette any more. There was no Wright or Bright to bollock me now. That all seemed like a long time ago. I looked at the number one peg with the growing realisation that my shirt would never hang on it. My frustration boiled over one day with a forward called Tony Finnan. Tony was hugely talented, but instead of working hard at being the best footballer he could be he was always messing around doing tricks and flicks and trying to chip me from forty yards. I got so angry with watching him waste his talent that I chased him out of the training ground and all the way up the road.

Ray Lewington had been ringing around to try and get me some football. Over Christmas and New Year I went on loan to Gillingham. Their goalkeeper had picked up an injury and they weren't sure if he would play. He did, so I kept the bench warm for a few weeks. Next stop on my mystery tour was Burnley at the end of January 1996. Their first-choice 'keeper was injured and they wanted a substitute while the reserve 'keeper played.

This was the first time I'd spent more than a day in the north. Burnley was a bit bleak but the people were very friendly. The club was a sleeping giant with fanatical supporters, and the stadium was excellent. Yeah, I thought, things could work out for me here. The manager, Jimmy Mullen, was getting a lot of abuse because the team was struggling in Division Two. Mullen liked me and was on the verge of playing me. With my debut just around the corner, Mullen and his wife visited a local takeaway one evening. They encountered some seriously pissed-off Burnley fans, one of whom waved a cigarette lighter at Mrs Mullen. Jimmy resigned the next day and his assistant, Clive Middlemass, took over. Clive didn't rate me, so when my month ran out I returned to Selhurst Park. 'Manager's wife set on fire' was a good one for my collection of Reasons Why My Career Isn't Taking Off.

When I got back to Palace, Dave Bassett was in charge. He had walked through the revolving door of the manager's office while I was at Burnley. Dave is one of football's great characters. Everyone has loads of hilarious stories about him. Well, everyone except me. I told Dave I needed to get away; he said he'd see what he could do. Later that day, reserve-team coach Steve Kember rang me. 'Mel Machin, the Bournemouth manager, has been on the phone,' he said. 'Can you go there tomorrow with a view to a permanent move?'

Bournemouth were mid-table in Division Two. I drove down next day, took part in a training session, and met Machin. He seemed all right, especially when he said the magic words 'first-team football'. There was nothing for me at Palace. There was no chance of breaking into the first team while Nigel Martyn was around. I'd been at the club for eight-and-a-half years, since I was a boy of fourteen, and I'd had six months of coaching. I was the second-longest-serving player and I'd never played a match.

So on 8 March 1996 I signed a two-and-a-half-year contract with Bournemouth. It was worth £500 a week, the same as I was on at Palace, rising to £550 in the last year. There was also a £6,000 signing-on fee, to be paid in three instalments. Ron Noades kept his word and gave me a free transfer. If Bournemouth sold me Palace would get a cut of the transfer fee.

The Palace lads were training when I went back to sort things out. One of the women who worked at the training ground gave me a card signed by everyone. Later on there was a disagreement over my club suit. I'd given it back but they couldn't find it, so £200 was deducted from my final wages.

Two months later Palace were beaten by Leicester in the Division One play-off final. Nigel Martyn joined Leeds United and Rhys Wilmot was released. Palace replaced them with Carlo Nash and Chris Day. Both made their first-team debuts within weeks of joining the club.

Five

LAST MINUTE, GREAT SAVE

Straight after signing my Bournemouth contract I bought a Mercedes 190. It was a few years old, but I felt like a king behind the wheel. For the first few months I drove down from London on Monday mornings and stayed in the Berkeley Hotel. The Berkeley was owned by a Bournemouth fan and he charged players only £20 a night.

As Bournemouth were mid-table it was a relatively relaxed environment to come into. It was a good opportunity to do what I'd always wanted – play first-team football and get some experience. I played the last thirteen matches of the 1995/96 season. My debut came at Hull. I was nervous but I played reasonably well in a 1-1 draw and enjoyed it. Three days later we went to Wrexham and were hammered 5-0. I created one of the goals when I smacked a clearance into their centre forward and the ball rebounded into the net. I wasn't a great goalkeeper by any means; I was just finding my feet in League football.

One of my first games was at Carlisle, the city that would have a massive impact on my life three years later. I can't honestly say it was love at first sight. The never-ending drive up the M6 was horrendous. It was only a few more miles to Scotland. When we got the fixture list the first thing everyone looked for was Carlisle away. We prayed for a Saturday match because if it was midweek we wouldn't have got back until five o'clock the next morning. Carlisle is where I argued with Mel Machin for the first time. We lost 4-0, which didn't help. One of the goals came from a free-kick. I lined my wall up, then Carlisle moved the ball. I thought the players in my wall would have the sense to move with it. They didn't. Machin wasn't happy and he blamed me.

The main difference between League and reserve-team football was tempo rather than quality. At Palace I had been competing against good players from teams like Arsenal and Spurs, but the pace of the game was sedate compared with Division Two. After years in the reserves suddenly every game mattered to more than one man and his dog. The results are on Teletext; there are match reports in the papers; every mistake suddenly means something. The chink in my armour was that I worried about that. I cared about people's attitudes to me. I wanted people to think I was a good 'keeper and to say good things. If someone had a pop at me, it really hurt. Most players can bury those thoughts, if they have them at all. To me, football was life and death.

I had a love-hate relationship with the game. Life was constantly up and down. When I'd played well I was on top of the world and everything was great; when I'd played badly I was shit and everything was wrong. They say you're only as good as your last game, and that's how I judged myself. I knew millions of people would love to have my job. I'd wanted it for most of my life. But when you're on the bus home after being stuffed 5-0, when you're sitting through hours of bitching and piss-taking, being a footballer becomes a chore. And yet at the same time I loved being part of the first team and being involved. I had a lot of good matches and made a lot of friends. Being praised when I'd played well made me feel good about myself. I started feeling I was going to make it.

Nothing was better than a really good save, when the blur of a ball would appear out of nowhere and my hand would somehow block it. The other team have been working all week to try and score, to try and beat my team, and I've just stopped them. The buzz comes in the split-second after, when everyone is looking at me and thinking they've just seen something unbelievable.

Bournemouth's home, Dean Court, was a battered old ground. The main terrace was closed for safety reasons and they couldn't afford to repair it. The disabled shelter was a shed with a bit of plastic on top. I wanted to build a new one for Iain but the club wouldn't spend the money because they were trying to get a new stadium. Mum brought Iain to home matches. The disabled shelter was behind the South End goal where I warmed up. Before any fans arrived I would wheel Iain into the middle of the goal and hit balls at him. He'd sit there laughing. The ground would fill up, and suddenly there'd be 5,000 people watching us. The South End fans knew he was my brother and they enjoyed it.

It was a different story with opposition supporters. Fans at nearly every away match, including children, spat and swore at me when I walked behind the goal to collect the ball. I could usually rise above it, but not always. During a game against Bristol City I spent ninety minutes listening to a man shouting obscenities about my family: 'Your mother gives blowjobs on Bournemouth beach!' A policeman five yards away did nothing. Eventually I snapped and gave this bloke a 'wanker' sign. After the match another policeman told me to watch it, or I could be charged with incitement.

I soon understood Eric Cantona's reaction that night at Selhurst Park a year earlier. Cantona is a proud man who did what many players have longed to do when they've been baited by some toerag. Youngsters could learn a lot about self-respect from Cantona. Not that kids learn from footballers. They copy their dads, and they're the ones screaming and swearing every Saturday.

Players find it hard to accept the fickleness of supporters. Players can be having personal problems, they might be playing with an injury, but lifelong fans, who you think would know about football, still slaughter their own player if he misses a tackle. As a group, fans are generally fair. But players only notice the obnoxious ones. We learn not to listen to them by ignoring all fans. After a few games for Bournemouth I stopped saying anything to away supporters, or even looking at them. That hurt, because I enjoyed the banter with fans.

After the summer break I came back for pre-season training looking forward to my first full campaign of League football. Mel Machin signed defenders Ian Cox and Jamie Vincent, who were good friends of mine from Crystal Palace. Bournemouth is the place to be in summer. We'd head straight down to the beach after training and think, 'We've landed on our feet here!'

The 1996/97 season brought us crashing back down to earth. Right from the start we were conceding goals and not scoring – never a great combination. In early September we lost 3-0 at home to Ipswich in the League Cup and the crowd got on my back. Four days later we played Crewe at home and lost 1-0. One of their forwards beat four players before smacking the ball in the corner of my goal. After the match Mel Machin had a go at me. He said I'd committed the goalkeeper's cardinal sin of conceding a goal at my near post. I tried to explain that it wasn't the near post because the forward was level with the middle of the goal when he struck the ball. But Machin always made his mind up there and then, even if the action was through a crowd of players fifty yards away. After away games he would walk down the bus, sit next to someone, and ask why they'd done something. The blame for a bad result was laid right there. Machin always sounded really weary with his dour Yorkshire accent. 'What happened there, son?' was a rhetorical question. You could have said, 'Well, boss, Mickey Mouse came down from Mars,' and he wouldn't have noticed.

You bring the best out of players by boosting their confidence, not by blaming them in front of their colleagues. If I felt unfairly criticised I'd stand my ground. Like most managers, Mel Machin hated that. Not having his authority questioned was more important than accepting there might be an alternative opinion.

Machin knew a lot of people in football. He was good at getting players. But once they were there he didn't know what do with them. They'd either perform or they were out. He was never going to take a young lad and make him a great footballer. In the past that didn't matter so much because most managers were the same. Now, with so many foreign managers here, people like Machin don't succeed any more.

In the following Monday's *Bournemouth Daily Echo*, Machin stated that Crewe's goal was my fault and that I wasn't prepared to accept responsibility for it. On the same day he signed Andy Marshall, Norwich City's reserve keeper, on a month's loan. 'I think you need a rest for a couple of games,' Machin told me. 'Work hard and you'll be back in the team.' I didn't argue. I worked really hard that month and played well in training. Andy Marshall trained at Norwich. He started training at Bournemouth, then he realised we didn't have a goalkeeping coach so he stayed in Norwich until Friday mornings.

Andy played the next five matches. I wouldn't be human if I hadn't felt a hint of satisfaction when Bournemouth lost four of them. He then had an England Under-21 game which coincided with the end of his loan period. I played in a 1-1 draw at Gillingham, happy to be back. On the Monday morning I arrived at the training ground. Andy Marshall was there. Machin had signed him for another month. I stormed off to see the chairman, Ken Gardner.

'I can't work with someone who says one thing and does another!' I told him.

'Mel signed Marshall without my knowledge,' said Gardner. 'I've told him he can't sign him again. Wait the month and you'll be back in the team.'

When the month was up, Marshall did indeed return to Norwich. Machin told the *Daily Echo* he was devastated that Marshall had gone back but Norwich needed him. A few days later, Andy Marshall went on loan to Gillingham.

After a few months at the Berkeley Hotel I'd begun renting a flat in Westbourne with Jamie Vincent. I was earning enough money to buy somewhere, but after being dropped that didn't seem the most sensible option. I didn't know if I would even see out my contract. Jamie became my best friend in football, even though we're very different people. He's laid back and doesn't let anything bother him. Neither of us was particularly house-proud and the flat never made it into *Ideal Homes*. The furniture was just a couple of beds and a television, but that didn't stop us having a good time – maybe too good.

During my last season at Palace I'd started going out with a girl called Carrie. I still saw her in London at weekends but during the week I was out and about in Bournemouth. It was the first time I'd lived away from home, let loose in a town full of clubs and bars and beautiful women. Carrie wanted to move to Bournemouth but I was enjoying myself too much without her. She had a beaten-up B-reg Ford Fiesta. I told her I didn't want her driving down because I was worried the car wouldn't make it. The truth is I just didn't want her around.

Before I moved to Bournemouth, I'd never gambled. I'd never even played a fruit machine. My first visit to Grosvenor House casino changed everything. I went one night with Bournemouth's assistant manager John Williams and a couple of former players. It was great. A tenner magically transformed into £20, then £50, then £150. One night I walked in with £40 and left an hour later with £1,100. That was the worst thing that could have happened. Money became easy. A lot of players, even in Division Two, were getting £30,000 signing-on fees and £2,000 a week. Some Fulham players were earning £10,000 a week. Suddenly my £500 seemed like I was being short-changed. I wanted more money; maybe I could win it. I wanted nicer clothes and a newer car. That's how I measured success, and had done ever since my YTS at Palace. The pros there used to turn up in their BMWs and Mercedes and designer suits. Any of the apprentices who had Armani jeans or jackets were regarded as top dogs. It was in your face non-stop.

Blackjack and poker were my games. I learned to love the ups and downs, the highs and lows, the excitement of the unpredictable. 'Last minute, great save' – it was that sort of mentality. As I sat there with the cards flying and the wheel spinning, it felt like I'd wandered into a James Bond film. The highs were phenomenal, like jumping into a cab with £5,000 in my pocket. Gambling gave me a buzz I didn't find in normal life. The only other place I found it was football.

It wasn't long before I owed thousands and had to resort to bank loans. I lost a month's wages in a couple of hours. Then I won three months' wages, and lost four months'. If I lost £1,000 I'd get out another £1,000 to chase it. When I had a big win that cleared my debts the relief was incredible. The heat was off. 'Right, I can get on with a normal life now.' Next week I'd go back and lose £5,000. People who don't gamble don't understand. 'How can you blow five grand? I couldn't afford to lose that kind of money!' But that's the kick. The likes of Paul Merson and Eidur Gudjohnsen can afford to lose when they're earning £40,000 a week. Unless you're gambling with something you can't afford to lose, it isn't gambling.

I'd get home from the casino at four o'clock in the morning and be up for training five hours later. After training I'd sleep until five in the afternoon then go back to the casino. There was a spell when I was drinking every night – not huge amounts, but still too much. You have to be so disciplined to get through the YTS and the early years as a professional. All my adult life and most of my childhood had been dedicated to football. When temptation came along I was ready to be tempted.

The funny thing was that this behaviour didn't seem to affect my performances. My lifestyle was balanced by the fact that I was playing regularly in the first team at last. After Andy Marshall returned to Norwich I played in Bournemouth's next eighty-eight games.

I can't excuse my off-field behaviour. All I can say is that Bournemouth and me were as bad as each other. The club wouldn't pay for a professional goalkeeping coach. I could see 'keepers like Richard Wright at Ipswich progressing because they had specialist coaches to pinpoint their weaknesses and work on them. At Arsenal, their former goalkeeper Bob Wilson was helping David Seaman become the best 'keeper in England. Meanwhile, Bournemouth employed a delivery driver called Clive. He played in goal for a local team and knew a bit about it. He meant well but he wasn't a proper coach. A goalkeeping coach should break your game down and make you realise things you didn't see before. The only way to do that is with someone who has played at the level you're playing at. Clive didn't have that insight, and he didn't feel comfortable criticising me because I was a professional. It might have been better if he was a full-time coach but he had to work elsewhere.

Clive would turn up on Monday and Thursday afternoons at three o'clock, after I'd been sitting around at the training ground for two hours, often shivering in cold, wet kit. I kept asking for a spare set but it never arrived. Most of my training was the same as the outfield players', as it had been at Palace. I couldn't really see how dribbling the ball around cones was going to help me stop shots and catch crosses. The raw materials were all there – I was 6ft 4in tall, agile, strong and eager to learn – but those qualities were never exploited. I'd never been taught how to get into the right position quickly, how to combat opponents who would block your path to crosses. There's only so much you can learn when someone is kicking the ball to you and you're catching it.

My enthusiasm on the training ground was at its greatest when it came to working with Bournemouth's younger players. Some of them were struggling to strike the ball as well as they could have. I'd take them aside, or they'd come to me because they'd seen me smacking the ball ninety yards. I've always had ideas about centre forward training because I know what goalkeepers don't like. The best thing a striker can do is hit the ball as quickly as possible before the 'keeper has time to prepare.

Some senior players and coaches ridiculed my involvement. You've got to be open-minded to learn, and a goalkeeper advising a forward was too much for some people to take in. Sean O'Driscoll, who was the club's youth-team manager, was all for it. He said, 'How come you train them so much better than you train yourself?' Rightly or wrongly, I thought it wasn't my job to train myself. I was waiting for coaches to come and coach me. I spent the first half of my career waiting to be taught how to be a goalkeeper.

Six

MONEY, LOVE AND WEMBLEY

You could never really call Bournemouth a glamour club. Their place in English football is Division Three at worst, Division One at best. As 1996 turned into 1997 they were right in the middle, coasting along in Division Two. One Friday morning at the end of January, the calm was shattered. The players were gathered together to hear some news: Bournemouth had been placed in receivership; the club owed £5 million.

We had known there were problems – wages were sometimes a week or two late – but we hadn't expected anything like this. Bournemouth wasn't perceived as a big-spending club but it had been living beyond its means for many years and losing nearly £1 million a season. Several clubs have gone into receivership or administration since then, but Bournemouth was one of the first. The previous two clubs with big financial problems, Aldershot and Maidstone, had both been forced to resign from the Football League. It looked as if Bournemouth would be next to disappear off the map.

The receiver, Alan Lewis, was now running the club on behalf of Lloyds Bank. Lloyds were the main creditors, and they wanted their money. Alan said he didn't know if we would be paid this month. There were a few murmurs of, 'Well, we're not gonna play then.' Being a bolshy sod, I stood up and said, 'Come on, fellas, we've got to keep going.' Next day we went to Bristol City and won 1-0. That was a big thing because there was a lot of rivalry between Bournemouth and City. We hadn't been playing well either, so it was a great result. The club picked up on that and said to the fans, 'These lads don't know if they're going to be paid. Get behind them and we can all help each other.' More than 8,000 turned up for the next home game against Blackpool because they thought it might be Bournemouth's last

League match. It was vital for the fans to show they wanted a club. If they weren't bothered, why should the receiver worry about trying to save it? Bournemouth is known as God's waiting room but it's actually a young town and the football club generates a lot of spirit.

I attended a couple of meetings as the players' representative. It wasn't easy listening. The club owed Lloyds nearly £2.5 million, and £650,000 to the taxman. The creditors were losing patience. We needed to raise £300,000 within a few weeks or be thrown out of the League. Sixteen staff were laid off to cut costs. A meeting for fans was arranged at the Winter Gardens. Alan Lewis was there with Mel Machin and Trevor Watkins, who was a lawyer and a fan. Alan was a Crystal Palace supporter, and a supporter of football in general. He didn't want Bournemouth to go to the wall. All the players were there, including Matty Holland, the club captain. Matty was the key figure for Mel Machin because the fans loved him. We called Matty 'Golden Bollocks'. On Monday mornings he'd have a cup of tea with Machin and a chat about Saturday's game. Machin would tell him what to tell the players and Matty never rocked the boat.

The Winter Gardens was packed with 3,000 people. The reception when we came down the aisles and onto the stage was unbelievable. The apprentices went around with buckets for donations and we raised more than £30,000 that night. Trevor Watkins and an accountant, Ken Dando, set up a trust fund. This led the fund-raising effort to buy the club from the receiver. Receivership had a positive effect on the team as it brought the players closer together. We socialised a lot anyway and the bonds grew stronger through this crisis. We lost just three of the season's last eighteen games and I kept ten clean sheets in thirteen matches. On our day we ripped teams to shreds. Off the field, players and fans didn't have a clue what was going on. All sorts of rumours were flying around.

Suddenly, salvation came. That summer the trust fund signed an agreement with the creditors and bought the club from the receiver. Trevor Watkins became chairman and Bournemouth became Europe's first community-owned football club. The supporters had done it, by turning up at the Winter Gardens, by coming to the matches, by using their passion to give people hope that maybe we could pull this off. Watkins went on to win BBC South Sports Personality of the Year. The players were less enthusiastic. We lost confidence in him because he made promises about contracts that he didn't always keep.

At the time, the fans were just happy that the club was safe. Since then, Bournemouth has hit further financial difficulties. The new constitution stated that no one could own more than ten per cent of the club, to stop any individual dictating its future. That's lovely if you've got ten millionaires, but lower-division clubs struggle to generate enough money to be self-sufficient. Within a few years, Bournemouth had run up debts of £5 million again.

In the summer of 1997, however, everything was rosy. Businesses were queuing up to support born-again Bournemouth and for the new season I was sponsored by SpecSavers; the commercial department thought that was very amusing. Mel Machin let me play up front in a friendly at local non-League side Bournemouth Sports. I scored a hat-trick, including a twenty-five-yard volley. In August we played a friendly at Dean Court against Manchester United. David Beckham picked the ball up on the halfway line, nutmegged John O'Neill and slapped it into the top corner from thirty yards. I waved at it as it went past me. On his *Beckham's Greatest Goals* video, he names that as the best goal he's scored in a friendly. I've played against Beckham three times and twice he's beaten me from outside the penalty area. If that isn't proof of his ability, I don't know what is.

Jamie Vincent moved out of our flat and in with his girlfriend. Matty Holland was transferred to Ipswich to bring in some much-needed money, so I moved into his flat with one of the other players, midfielder Leo Cotterell. Football was fine. I'd been playing well and was a fans' favourite, but my gambling overshadowed everything. I was sliding deeper and deeper into debt. One night at the casino I met Claudia. She was twenty years old, a model from a wealthy family. That was good enough for me. I split up with Carrie. When I had to move out of Matty Holland's flat, Claudia and I moved in together.

In December, Bournemouth played Bristol City at home in the second round of the FA Cup. The match was shown live on Sky. City were on a nine-game winning run and needed one more win to break their club record. We beat them 3-1 and I was named Man of the Match. I played out of my skin and the supporters never forgot that. During a break in play a fan ran on the pitch. He was wearing a T-shirt that said 'Kiss My Glass!'

The fans used to chant, 'Jimmy's fucking mental!', which I like to think was a compliment. The supporters appreciated my efforts to create some fun. I developed a pre-match routine with Bournemouth's mascot, Cherry Bear. I'd kick the ball at him, he would push me, and I'd chase him. One day I rugby-tackled him and his head fell off. He was on the ground yelling, 'Don't let the kids see my face!' The kids loved it. They didn't want to see Cherry Bear handing out sweets, they wanted to see him having a fight with the goalkeeper!

If the ball was passed back to me and I was under a bit of pressure, I had the confidence to dribble it round an opposition striker and pass it. The ball was never taken off me but I was classed as dodgy by the management. I was showing composure and strength of character, but Mel Machin hated it with a passion. In one match against Burnley, Jamie Vincent knocked the ball back to me at a tight angle and their striker came flying in. Instead of hoofing the ball out of play, I dragged it back across the goal line and cleared it. I once dribbled all the way to the halfway line. We were playing York at home. I parried the ball on the edge of my penalty area and it broke loose ten yards outside the box. I ran out and dribbled it up the pitch. A York player tried to tackle me, so I knocked it between his legs and kept running. It put the fear of God into the fans, but they loved it.

Suddenly I was ten yards from the halfway line and it was two on two. I was going to take on the last centre-back. I'm quite quick, so I thought, 'Sod it – I'll run with it.' I was facing their goal and he was facing me. If I'd knocked it past him he would never have caught me. But I knew the reaction I'd have got from Mel Machin. I was going to run past the dugout, and Machin would probably have tripped me up. So I passed it, and I've always regretted that. There was no reason to pass. I could have run all the way up the pitch. It could have been one of the great moments in football. But the game stopped me. Not the fans, but the management.

I did make it to the opposition penalty area twice in a Bournemouth shirt, though. Against Watford we were a goal down when we won a corner in the last minute. I ran upfield, midfielder John Bailey crossed it and I jumped with their goalkeeper. He dropped the ball and someone lashed in the equaliser. I was about to celebrate but the linesman gave a goal kick: the ball had gone out of play from the corner. The other time was an FA Cup third-round match at Huddersfield. We were losing 1-0 and I came up for a last-minute corner. The ball was whipped in but it hit the first defender and that was that. Instead of being the hero I had to leg it back to my goal.

There were other times when I'd be shaping to run upfield and Machin would scream at me to get back. If I saved a penalty or made a great stop my teammates would urge me to calm down. They knew I'd be chasing the ball everywhere. Nothing compares to the adrenaline you get through sport. Fans feel it too. They want to be entertained. They don't want football to be a business with all the joy sucked out of it.

However, at AFC Bournemouth, business often had to come before pleasure. The club needed to make payments to the bank so every now and then they had to sell a player. Matty Holland was the first, and there have been a few more since. When Matty left, I took over as the club's Professional Footballers' Association (PFA) representative. I liked the thought of players having the union. Some of the younger lads came to me with any problems. I enjoyed helping them sort out their pensions and talking about their future.

Eddie Howe was an England Under-21 international who was a fantastic prospect and had become a regular at centre-back. Eddie came to me and said the club had offered him a long-term deal. I said, 'Before you sign anything, ring the PFA and they'll help you negotiate.' He spoke to them and they said the contract was okay. Two weeks later Eddie said, 'I've signed the contract but I don't think I'm happy with it.' The club had him on a six-year deal and the most he could earn was about £700 a week. I phoned the PFA and asked what had happened. They looked into it but it was too late.

Around this time Gary O'Reilly, my former Crystal Palace colleague, asked if I'd be interested in having him as my agent. He was working for Mark Goldberg, who had a sports agency and would later buy Palace. I wasn't a favourite of Mel Machin's so it seemed sensible to get someone working for me, especially as my contract was due to run out a few months later, in June 1998. Negotiating isn't my strong point because I don't feel comfortable discussing money. Things had gone quiet with the Stellar Agency so I signed with Gary, as did Jamie Vincent and Eddie Howe.

Gary approached Mel Machin about Eddie Howe's contract. Machin told him to get out. He then told Eddie that he would review his contract if he got rid of Gary, which suggested to me that Eddie had been given a duff contract to start with. Because I'd introduced Gary to the club, Machin and Trevor Watkins saw me as a trouble-maker, but I was only trying to look after the young players, as a PFA rep should. If things are done fairly there doesn't have to be trouble.

None of this helped my case for a new contract. At the beginning of 1998 I asked for £700 a week and a £10,000 signing-on fee because I wanted to buy a flat. I was one of the most experienced players and some were earning £1,500 a week. Machin and Watkins were never available to discuss it. The following year, Watkins wrote a book about his involvement with Bournemouth. He said he and Machin hadn't wanted to keep me, but they'd decided not to tell me. He questioned whether I would have tried my hardest if I'd known I wouldn't be staying at Bournemouth. It's a good job Watkins never said that to my face. I wasn't always brilliant, but I always tried. If Machin or Watkins had told me that my contract would not be renewed, I could have made plans. Instead my life was in limbo. My form wavered because I was insecure over not knowing if I'd still be at Dean Court for 1998/99. The tension over my contract and my PFA involvement was affecting my relationship with Machin. We played Plymouth at home and he had a go at me at half-time. I walked out and sat in the boot room. I didn't want to argue and I wasn't going to sit there and take it so there didn't seem to be many other options.

Around the middle of that 1997/98 season I had spoken to Alan Smith, my former Crystal Palace manager. He was now in charge of Fulham's youth academy. Fulham were a Second Division club, like Bournemouth. Unlike Bournemouth, however, they had recently been bought by Harrods owner Mohammed al Fayed. Money was not a problem there. I asked Alan if I could work at Fulham's training ground with Peter Bonetti, who was coaching the club's goalkeepers. Alan asked the manager, Kevin Keegan, and he very kindly said it was okay. Bournemouth had Wednesdays off, so I trained with Fulham every Wednesday for the next few months. I didn't tell anyone at Bournemouth because they would have felt it made them look bad, which it did. During this period Bournemouth played at Fulham's Craven Cottage, one Tuesday night in February. I played really well and we won 1-0, making their multi-million-pound stars look average. Next morning I turned up at Fulham, bright and breezy, ready for training. Ray Wilkins, Fulham's assistant manager, took one look at me then turned to Alan Smith and said, 'Is he taking the piss?'

Bournemouth's good form that season was not confined to the League. The Auto Windscreens Shield, or the LDV Vans Trophy as it later became, is a cup competition for teams from Divisions Two and Three. After wins in the first three rounds we found ourselves in the southern-area final. Our opponents in this two-legged tie were Walsall. At stake was a first trip to Wembley in Bournemouth's ninety-nine-year history and the chance to bring the club some much-needed money. We won the away leg 2-0 and I played well. But the home leg, on 17 March, was my worst game for Bournemouth.

At half-time it was 0-0. We were forty-five minutes from Wembley and a fairytale recovery from the previous year's problems. Then I almost ruined everything. At the start of the second half I misjudged a shot from the edge of the penalty area, which dipped under my hand and into the goal. A few minutes later I came charging out to claim the ball and didn't get near it. Walsall striker Roger Boli knocked it around me and tapped it into the net. Walsall were level.

A Walsall own goal gave us an aggregate 3-2 lead. Then they equalised again. With a few minutes left our French defender Franck Rolling raced forward and hit the winning goal. Bournemouth were at Wembley, no thanks to me.

After the final whistle I couldn't speak. I'd almost cost the club their place at the national stadium. Maybe I was upset because I'd almost cost myself the chance to play there. Maybe this was a selfish thought. Mel Machin gathered the team together in the dressing room to congratulate them on their fantastic achievement. I grabbed my clothes, drove home and went straight to bed. That night an action replay of my mistakes ran through my head over and over again. It's funny how easy it is to remember them compared to the saves.

The supporters knew that Machin and me weren't getting on. A fan rang a local radio station and asked, 'Is Jimmy Glass throwing games?' I was devastated. I kept twenty-two clean sheets that season. In the previous four matches of the Auto Windscreens Shield I hadn't conceded a goal. It hammered home what I'd always known: you're only as good as your last game.

A journalist told me that Machin had rung West Ham and Chelsea to see if he could sign a 'keeper on loan for the rest of the season. Gary

O'Reilly asked Trevor Watkins what was happening. Watkins said, 'Jimmy's playing at Wembley.' That was all I wanted to hear. But I was resigned to leaving as Machin and Watkins weren't even speaking to me by then.

One of my last games for Bournemouth was at Carlisle in March 1998, a year before I went there on loan. That's the only match I've ever flown to. To avoid the never-ending coach journey the club chartered a plane with some fans. We flew to Newcastle and drove across to Carlisle. We were winning 1-0 when Carlisle were awarded a last-minute penalty. Their striker Ian Stevens smacked the ball low to my right. I had it covered, but in the end it only clipped the post anyway. I was gutted that he didn't get it on target because I would have saved it.

Bournemouth's first visit to Wembley came on Sunday 19 April 1998. The night before, we stayed at the Hilton in Wokingham. Next morning we were driven down Wembley Way. It was packed with fans. This was also the Wembley debut of our opponents, Grimsby Town, so there was a fantastic atmosphere in the stadium. In the dressing room we could hear the songs and chants of 63,000 people. It was the biggest crowd I'd ever played in front of, the biggest I ever will. Then there was the television audience watching live on Sky.

As we walked down the tunnel into the most famous arena in football, I tried to put my jersey on. It was too small. The kit man had put the wrong one out. I had to run back and find another and I was still dragging it over my head as I finally emerged into the stadium.

The Bournemouth fans were at the tunnel end, all 34,000 of them. I walked along the pitch looking for Iain and Mum. They were supposed to be right at the front but I couldn't see them. I spent the next five minutes worrying about them. Maybe it was a defence mechanism to avoid thinking about the game. It's a great feeling to play at Wembley – afterwards. At the time we were shitting ourselves. Everyone was determined not to look stupid. All matches are like that to an extent, but Wembley magnifies everything.

The game kicked off. After half an hour there was a mix up in the Grimsby defence. The ball broke loose and John Bailey knocked it in: 1-0 to Bournemouth. We held out until fifteen minutes from full time. A cross came over to my far post and Grimsby winger Kingsley Black headed the ball down from point-blank range. It hit the inside of my leg and went in: 1–1. With just a few seconds left Grimsby's John McDermott unleashed a fierce shot that flew towards the right-hand corner of my goal. I flung myself full length and tipped it round the post.

The match moved into golden-goal extra time, otherwise known as 'next goal wins'. The first half of extra time came and went. I was looking forward to a penalty shoot-out. I wanted to be a hero. Then, with a few minutes left, the ball was played into my penalty area. I ran out to dive on it but one of my defenders, Ian Cox, touched it back to me. It was just a slight touch but it counted as a back-pass so I couldn't use my hands. I lunged on the ball with my chest and it was scrambled out for a corner. It looked awful. The corner came in. Grimsby midfielder Wayne Burnett was unmarked at the far post. He volleyed the ball across me into the corner of the goal. Game over.

I lay face down in my six-yard box. There are photographs of us in the goalmouth, some flat out on the grass, some standing with their hands on their hips, some with their heads in their hands.

A Grimsby player picked me up. 'Come on, son,' he said. 'If you hadn't made that save we wouldn't have had extra time.' I don't know if that was his way of saying the winning goal was my fault for conceding the corner. The Bournemouth fans were quiet for a few seconds, then they erupted. They were just happy to be there, whatever the result. They saw the day as a bit of payback for their support the previous year. That was the lovely thing about it: the fans saved the club and the next season we took them to Wembley. One sour point was that Mel Machin didn't bring Franck Rolling off the subs bench – bearing in mind he had scored the goal that got us there. Franck was very disheartened by that and he left the club soon afterwards. Before the game I'd planned to wheel Iain around the pitch if we won. I tried to do it anyway, but a steward wouldn't let me.

Next day the newspaper reports said, 'Glass spilled the back pass'. How can you spill a back pass? You're not allowed to pick it up. Some players could have let it go but I wanted to say, 'I couldn't pick it up – there was nothing I could do! I was stuck!' To cap it all, Grimsby's equaliser was listed as, 'Glass, 80 minutes, own goal'. I had made history: the first goalkeeper to score an own goal at Wembley.

When I got the internet a couple of years later I logged on to some Bournemouth websites and read the emails from that day. Some fans were complimentary. It was nice to think that not everyone blamed me. I enjoy Wembley more when I look back on it. It was a good day, and that's what I take from it now. Whatever happens, there'll always be another game.

My last match at Dean Court was against Burnley on 25 April. We won 2–1. A disabled kid called Sean went to every Bournemouth home game. He took a shine to me and he always wanted to give me a hug. Early in the season, Sean had asked if he could have my goalie top and gloves. I said I needed the gloves but he could have my top. At the end of the Burnley match there was a pitch invasion. All the players sprinted for the tunnel while I headed down the middle of the pitch to the disabled shelter. I gave Sean my top and applauded him. The fans on the South End clapped. It was a nice way to say goodbye.

The following Saturday we were at Millwall for the final game of the season. When I ran out some Bournemouth fans dropped a banner over the away end: 'Good luck, Jimmy. Thanks for everything.' We were winning 2–1 in the last minute when I made a good save to tip the ball round the post for a corner. Thousands of Millwall fans swarmed onto the pitch. The referee took the teams off and made us wait in the tunnel. He said to me, 'When they take the corner, I want you to catch it then I'll blow the final whistle.' I thought, 'Yeah, it's that easy.' We went back on and the corner came over. I caught it and sprinted down the pitch with the ball in my hands. Everybody was staring at me – the referee hadn't blown his whistle. I just kept running.

Bournemouth finished four points short of a play-off position, which was quite an achievement for a club that had come so close to extinction the previous year. After the game I was in the directors' bar with Jamie Vincent and my parents. A chap came in with a bottle of whisky and said, 'That's from all the South End.' Mum started crying. I knew the fans respected my efforts for Bournemouth, even if not everyone else did.

As a reward for taking the club to Wembley we went to the USA for ten days and played three matches. Midfielder Jason Brissett didn't turn up so I was in a room on my own. Halfway through the stay, Trevor Watkins approached me and said, 'You're going to have to move out of your room. It's costing money. We'll put a camp-bed in one of the other rooms.'

'That's a bit unfair, Trev. I don't want to spend five days on a camp-bed in someone else's room.'

He didn't say anything. I went out for the afternoon, and when I got back my room was empty. Assistant manager John Williams had gone in there, put all my things in my suitcase and stuck it on a camp-bed in one of the other rooms. My ticket home got lost in the process and I had to pay for another. I found Trevor Watkins in the bar, and I let rip as he sat there with his mouth open. I may have gone over the top, but I knew this was my farewell to Bournemouth.

Seven

DOG SHIT PARK

Three clubs were interested in me: Cambridge United and Millwall of the Second Division, and First Division Swindon Town. Swindon was my first choice. Their manager was former Liverpool and England midfielder Steve McMahon. My agent, Gary O'Reilly, spoke to Steve while I went on holiday to Cyprus with Claudia. I couldn't relax because nothing had been sorted so I came back early to see Steve. He'd watched me at Bournemouth and was very keen. He said, 'I can't guarantee first-team football but you've got a good chance.' Swindon's previous number one, Fraser Digby, had just left. Frank Talia, the reserve keeper, had been injured for most of the previous season.

I thought this would be the pay day I'd been waiting for to clear my gambling debts, which had reached £15,000, but Steve said Swindon didn't pay signing-on fees. Even so, I signed a four-year contract worth £45,000 in the first year, rising by £5,000 in each of the following three years. The Bosman ruling meant Bournemouth didn't receive a penny for me; money that used to go to clubs in transfer fees was now going to players in wages. Although it was good money, nearly twice what I was on at Bournemouth, I was still disappointed not to receive a signing-on fee.

It soon emerged that Swindon had big financial problems, mainly because they had spent the previous few years agreeing to players' wage demands. I was caught up in the climate of the time. Competition in football doesn't end on the pitch. You're constantly looking at what other people have got and wondering if they deserve it. Frank Talia was on more money than me, even though he'd played fewer League games. Did that mean Swindon thought he was a better goalkeeper than me? If you're not a strong character in terms of focus, that stuff can play on your mind.

★

From my first day in Bournemouth I'd had a good feeling about the town. Swindon felt different. It wasn't a bad place, just nothing special. Swindon didn't feel like a football town as Bournemouth had or as Carlisle would. But the excitement of moving to a First Division club glossed over any concerns. I rented a house with Claudia and hoped for the best.

Swindon Town were paying the price for previous successes. In 1990 Ossie Ardiles had led Swindon into the old First Division. It had then emerged that two years previously the chairman had bet £5,000 of the club's money on Swindon losing an FA Cup tie. The club admitted thirty-eight breaches of Football League rules and were denied their place in the top flight. They finally made it in 1993 under Glenn Hoddle, but he left to manage Chelsea and Swindon went straight down again. The club had been saddled with players on Premiership contracts and was still suffering the consequences. The major share-holder, Sir Seton Wills, was keeping Swindon afloat.

When I arrived the club had narrowly escaped relegation to Division Two for the second year running. It wasn't hard to see why they were struggling. We trained at the back of Swindon's County Ground stadium on an area the players had christened Dog Shit Park. The goals leaned backwards and had no nets. The pitch was water-logged. But these were the least of our worries. You didn't need Stephen Hawking to tell you how Dog Shit Park got its nickname. It seemed like the entire population of Wiltshire walked their dogs on it. There was shit everywhere. I used to land in it all the time. Players would move the goals to where there was most of it. Sometimes they'd even rub the ball in it.

So this was the First Division. Managers expect excellence on a football pitch. Fine, but how about giving us the facilities to achieve it? It's like giving a carpenter a blunt saw and a broken hammer and asking him to make a Chippendale cabinet. It's such a false economy. Clubs might save a few quid with crap facilities but they pay for it with their players' morale.

If the pitches are boggy or the nets are ripped, I'll say so. If the train-ing balls are crap, I'll say so. Crap training balls nearly cost me my career, so I think I'm entitled to an opinion. All I'm trying to do is make my team – their team – better. But as soon as you speak out it goes against you. You're a whinger or a troublemaker. My complaints got the usual reaction: 'Yeah, whatever. Get on with it.'

Pre-season went well. I played most of the friendlies and conceded only one goal. Frank Talia got fit and it was touch and go who would start the first game at Sheffield United. In the dressing room at Bramall Lane, Steve McMahon announced that Frank was playing. Swindon lost 2-1. During the week we had a League Cup tie against Wycombe. I played and we won 2-1. Thinking, 'You don't change a winning team', I expected to play against Sunderland on the Saturday. Frank played. Frank was a larger-than-life Australian. I liked him a lot, which made it difficult to watch him play. I caught myself hoping he'd make a balls-up so I could get in the team.

At least Swindon had a goalkeeping coach. But Peter Williams was similar to Clive at Bournemouth: he knew a lot of theory but lacked authority because he hadn't played professional football.

Playing in the reserves was a novelty after two years of first-team football. But as the weeks passed I started getting annoyed with myself and Swindon. I couldn't find my form. We lost one reserve game 4-0. Before the next match, against QPR, I thought, 'I'll try really hard tonight and do everything right.' We lost 5-0 and I had an absolute stinker. Vinny Jones scored from thirty-five yards, so it wasn't a great game for me. I came in at half-time, 3-0 down and furious. I'd gone to Swindon thinking it was a step up but I was sliding backwards. Ross McClellan, the reserve-team manager, said, 'What are you playing at, Jimmy?' Then Steve McMahon stepped in: 'You're playing crap! You're just shit!'

I took my boots off and threw them on the floor, then I started taking off my gloves. If Steve had put my contract in front of me I would have torn it up. 'I've had enough of you!' I said. 'I don't even respect you!'

Steve looked a bit taken aback. 'What about Peter Williams?' he asked. 'Do you like Peter?'

'Of course I like Peter.'

He turned to Peter. 'Peter, will you fucking tell him?'

After the game, Ross said, 'Go home and calm down. You got excited in the heat of the moment, so did Steve.'

I went home and thought about it. Why should footballers have abuse hurled at them by their employer? It wouldn't happen in any other job. But I had to apologise because you don't speak to a manager that way. Next morning I said sorry. I told Steve I wasn't enjoying life at Swindon and was pissed off about not playing. He told me to have a week off, get my head right and start again. I went home to London, had a couple of rounds of golf and chilled out.

On the Saturday, Frank Talia broke his nose in a match at Bristol City. I wasn't due back until Wednesday but I went in on Monday because Swindon had a home game against Oxford the following night. We won 4-1 and I played really well. There was a good chance I would have played the following Saturday, but in the last minute I went up for a cross and an Oxford player came flying into me. I had a dead leg. Frank was recalled. A few days later I was fit but Frank kept his place.

Then Swindon suffered a couple of heavy defeats and I thought I might get another chance. Steve McMahon was under a lot of pressure, and an on-pitch 'McMahon out' sit-in after a 4-1 home defeat by Watford in mid-September prompted him to resign. The club was in a real mess financially and going nowhere fast, but the buck stopped with Steve. Peter Williams was the first casualty of the cost-cutting. He'd only been at Swindon for a month. Mike Walsh, the assistant manager, was put in temporary charge of the team.

I came in one day for a reserve game against Gillingham. 'All right, Jim?' said Mike. 'By the way, you're playing the last fifteen minutes up front.' The reserves were struggling to find enough forwards. Mike had spoken to Steve Coppell and Steve said, 'Why don't you play Jimmy Glass as a striker?'

With fifteen minutes to go, one of our strikers was taken off and replaced by our substitute goalkeeper. I came out of goal, swapped my green jersey for a red one, and jogged upfield. Jim Stannard in the Gillingham goal couldn't believe his eyes. People thought it was a joke. Then I started running past them. Players tend not to like that. It's a bit of a wake-up call for defenders when the opposition goalkeeper comes flying past. I picked the ball up on the wing, cut inside and hit a shot that was deflected wide. Gillingham started shutting me down a bit quicker after that. It's hard for a forward to come on for the last fifteen minutes and get with the pace of the game, never mind a goalkeeper. If you're going to do it, why not start with me up front or bring me on at half-time? But at least Mike Walsh tried it.

Steve McMahon's replacement was an old Swindon hero, Jimmy Quinn. Quinny had started his playing career at the County Ground and had another spell there in the mid-1980s, scoring plenty of goals as he did throughout a career which included 40 caps for Northern Ireland. Swindon was his second management job; he had been player-manager at Reading and was then Barry Fry's assistant at Peterborough. I was glad when Quinn came to Swindon. I'd met him at Bournemouth and I thought he might give me a chance.

It was easy to see why Jimmy Quinn had been such a successful player. He used to say, 'I'd sell my granny for a goal.' His intense will to win wasn't always pretty. In training he tackled his players as if they were bitter enemies rather than allies. One Saturday, Frank Talia had a bad game. On the bus home I was playing cards with Quinn and Mike Walsh when Quinn said to me, 'Hammer Frank and I'll play you next week,' because I'd never criticised any of the lads in front of him.

In January 1999 we played Bury at home. During the warm-up I was hitting shots at Frank. I smacked one ball and it soared past him towards the away end, where it smashed into the face of a teenage boy in a wheelchair. Bloody hell! I ran over. The boy's mouth was full of blood. Tears were rolling down his cheeks. His mum tried to reassure him, and me. She told me he was called Brian. I got changed and came out to see them. They weren't there: a St John's Ambulance man told me they'd sent Brian to hospital. I wasn't on the bench that day so I ran to my car and drove to the hospital up the road. Brian and his mum were in casualty. He had a bloodshot eye and bruising. After he'd been treated I took them back to the ground and we watched the second half together. Brian really touched me. He reminded me of my little brother. He kept chattering away about football with a completely innocent love of the game.

On Monday, Jimmy Quinn called me in. 'You were seen leaving the ground after kick-off,' he said.

I explained what had happened and that I'd had to go to the hospital.

'Couldn't you have sent someone else?'

Claudia and I weren't getting on too well. We decided to buy a house together, which was a big gamble even by my standards – maybe that commitment would make things better. I was twenty-five, she was twenty-one. We tried to live together as adults, thinking we knew what we wanted from life when we didn't know anything. Sometimes I regret having had girlfriends and not concentrating on football. But you've got to live.

I was still gambling, albeit in fits and starts, depending on how happy I was. If I was pissed off I would retreat to the casino. When Claudia was away I sometimes drove into London to gamble and got back at five in the morning before going in for training. Some days I'd have thousands of pounds in my goalie bag on the training pitch. Let's see, towel, spare gloves, £4,000 in cash...

I don't know if that level of gambling is as widespread among footballers as people seem to think. I didn't recognise the signs in anyone else, and I probably would have done, being so close to it myself. Gambling was part of the culture but most people didn't embrace it as wholeheartedly as me. At all my clubs the players had card games on the coach, mainly as a way of beating boredom. We played with pennies, but they represented pounds. If a manager sees 1,000 pennies on a table, he's not bothered; if he sees 1,000 pound coins, he might not be too happy. I once lost £600 playing three-card brag on the bus to an away game. The bloke who won it from me bought a patio. He said he named it after me.

Ever since my schooldays I'd never felt I fitted in anywhere. I'd created this lairy 'Jimmy Glass' character as a way of being one of the gang, and gambling was part of that persona. On the bus, when players were betting £1, I'd come along with £20. I thought that was the only way people might see me as exciting. In the boyish mentality of footballers, being known as a gambler has the same ring as 'He's a drinker' or 'He shags loads of birds'. One morning I showed some of the lads my previous night's winnings. Centre-back Brian Burrows smiled. 'That's all very well,' he said, 'but I bet you don't tell us when you lose.'

My financial acumen was nearly as bad as Mark Goldberg's. Goldberg had blown millions after buying Crystal Palace. Midway through the 1998/99 season I had to find a new agent when his firm went bust. I owed them £3,000, so that was quite handy. I employed the PFA as my new agents. They have a finger in all the pies and I trusted them to know what was going on.

Swindon's first team was still losing but my form improved and the reserves started to win. In the absence of a goalkeeping coach since Peter Williams' departure, I spent most training sessions playing left-back. We had three goalkeepers and Jimmy Quinn had sussed that I could play outfield. One morning I went to cross the ball and felt a pain in my knee. I'd torn my cartilage and was out for two months.

By the time it healed it was the end of March and Swindon were hovering around the relegation zone. Frank Talia hadn't been playing well, so Jimmy Quinn dropped him and put me in against QPR, for only my third game as a Swindon player. The first half was goalless; in the second half Swindon collapsed and we lost 4-0. I was on the wrong end of a bad team, as Frank had been. He was struggling because his confidence had suffered.

I kept my place for the next match, at home to promotion-chasing Ipswich. In the first minute one of our defenders handled the ball in the box and was sent off. Ipswich scored the penalty and ran away with the game. Someone trod on my ankle for the second goal and I couldn't put any weight on it, but we didn't have a 'keeper on the bench so I had to carry on. Things like that tend to get forgotten when you lose 6-0.

After the match my ankle had swollen to twice the size of my head, and my head is pretty big. Jimmy Quinn didn't mention my injury to the press; he told them he was dropping me. It added to my feeling that Quinny still had the dog-eat-dog mentality that had propelled him through his playing career. Anyone who made him look bad, even one of his own players, was left to fend for themselves. The example he set was 'every man for himself'. Team spirit was a crutch for the weak. We were all individuals.

For the next fortnight I had treatment on my ankle. My first day back training was on Dog Shit Park, where the players were doing kick-ups and headers to keep warm. I was never one to juggle the ball twenty-seven times and do a backflip. To me, it all depends on who puts the ball in the net the most or who keeps it out the most. Perhaps sensing my lack of enthusiasm, Jimmy Quinn turned to me and said, 'You don't inspire me.' I was puzzled. But after what had happened at Bournemouth, and with Steve McMahon, I thought, 'Maybe I shouldn't get angry. Maybe I shouldn't answer back.' So I didn't. I didn't say anything. That was the point in my career when I stopped standing up for myself. Looking back, I wish I'd said, 'You're the manager, Jim. Inspiring people is your job.' But I didn't want to rock the boat. I was tired of standing up for what I believed in only to be shat on by players and managers. I'd be looking for someone to stand up with me and nobody would.

Next morning Quinn called me in to his office. 'Carlisle have been on the phone,' he said.

Eight

CONFERENCE CALLING

Carlisle needed a goalkeeper for their last three games of the 1998/99 season. The transfer deadline had passed a few weeks earlier but clubs can sign a 'keeper after the deadline if they find themselves without one, as I'd found to my cost a few years earlier when Alan Smith had brought in Neil Sullivan for Crystal Palace's last match. Carlisle's goalkeeper had been a loan signing from Derby County and had just been recalled.

'Do you fancy it?' asked Jimmy Quinn.

My first thought was the same as when I used to check the fixture list at Bournemouth: 'Carlisle — that's miles away!' They were also in Division Three, quite a step down from Swindon, but I wanted to play. I didn't much care where it was.

My confidence had taken a hammering after conceding ten goals in two games then missing a fortnight's training. Going to Carlisle would be a chance to get something out of the season, to play a few matches and hopefully help restore my self-belief.

I phoned Nigel Pearson, Carlisle's manager. 'I'm up for it,' I said. 'When do you want me?'

Nigel sounded impressed by my enthusiasm. I arranged to turn up for training on Thursday morning, in two days' time. The next call was to Dad, explaining my latest career move and telling him to expect me in a couple of hours, en route to Carlisle.

When I strolled in, Dad looked at me as if I was mad. 'You do realise Carlisle are in a bit of trouble?' he asked. He punched a few buttons on the remote control and the Division Three table appeared on Teletext. Carlisle were second from bottom, three points ahead of Scarborough. Scarborough had two games in hand. I sat down and stared at the screen. My new club were favourites to be relegated from the Football

League to the dreaded Conference. No wonder Nigel Pearson had been impressed by my enthusiasm.

The drop into non-League is the steepest in sport. Communities lose part of their identity. Footballers are branded for life with the F-word: failure! What was I doing? I was a First Division player – one small step below the Premiership! It might have been one giant leap for Swindon Town's reserve goalkeeper, but the chance to progress was always there. Not in the Conference. That's where League clubs go to die. What if I messed up? What if I dropped a corner or spilled a shot in the last match? I would be the man who relegated Carlisle. But I'd made a promise. There was no backing out.

Next day I said, 'Right, Dad. I'm off.'

'Are you sure?'

'Yeah. I'm sure.'

For 300 miles of motorway I tried to think positively. Come on, this is an adventure! How many people would go to Carlisle for three games that could send them out of the League? How many people are that stupid? BBC Radio Five's featured match was the Champions League semi-final second leg between Juventus and Manchester United. United reached the final with a late winner from Andy Cole. I thought of him at Villa Park four years earlier, in his trenchcoat and beret. Our careers hadn't followed quite the same path since our difference of opinion, but Cole and Man United didn't matter to me now. I was focused on a far more important match: Scarborough *v.* Leyton Orient in Division Three. After five minutes Scarborough took the lead. 'Great – I'll arrive in Carlisle just in time to see my new club hit the bottom of the League.' At ten o'clock I left the M6 and checked in at the Forté Posthouse hotel. Scarborough had lost 3-1.

Next morning I drove to Brunton Park. Carlisle United didn't look like a club on the brink of non-League football. How many non-League clubs have a 16,000 capacity and a 6,000-seat stand? I had a chat with Nigel Pearson and signed my loan forms. Nigel had enquired about other goalkeepers but for some reason they hadn't exactly been falling over themselves to come up to Carlisle. I was very impressed with Nigel. He was under huge pressure but he managed not to show it. His message was simple: 'Right, you're here. Let's do the job.' I was interviewed by the local press. 'Pressure is a funny thing,' I said. 'The only pressure you are really under is what you put on yourself. I didn't put the club in this position but I'll do my best to get them out of it.'

The players were preparing for Saturday's home game against Darlington. I went out to meet them and was introduced to Paul Heritage, the reserve-team goalkeeper. He was injured, which was why the Football League had allowed Carlisle to bring in another 'keeper. Paul filled me in about the situation at Carlisle. No one had expected them to be in this position. They had gone down from Division Two the previous year and were among the favourites for promotion, but losing had become a habit they couldn't break. They had won just two of their last seventeen matches. The team was in freefall. Only one player at the club had cost a transfer fee; the rest were mainly loan signings and inexperienced youngsters.

For most of the season Hull, Hartlepool and Scarborough had been the relegation favourites. Hull had new owners and new players and were safe. Hartlepool's form had improved dramatically and they were almost out of danger. In February, Scarborough had appointed Colin Addison as manager and they had started winning. Carlisle had been swallowed by the pack. I said to Paul Heritage: 'They're in a bit of a mess here, aren't they?'

'You've got nothing to worry about,' he replied. 'They won't blame you if they go down. And if they stay up, you'll be the hero.'

'What if I score the winner?'

People don't believe me when I tell them that but Paul will confirm it. That was the romantic in me. You have to truly believe in football; otherwise it can destroy you, like it has a lot of players.

I didn't know much about Carlisle United then but I've learned a lot more since. Carlisle had been in the Football League for seventy-one years. Bill Shankly started his managerial career there. They were Peter Beardsley's first League club. Carlisle had a bit of history. They hadn't always been crap. Twenty-five years before I arrived at Brunton Park, Carlisle had arrived in the old First Division. Remember Denis Law's back-heeled goal for Manchester City at Old Trafford, the goal that relegated Manchester United? The club who replaced Manchester United in the top flight was Carlisle. That was their first season in football's elite. Everyone expected them to go straight back down, then they won their first three matches to go top of the Football League. In August 1974, Carlisle United were the best team in England.

But the wins dried up and the fairytale faded. Carlisle were relegated. They spent most of the next decade in the old Second Division, facing teams like Newcastle, Chelsea and Leeds. Fast-forward a few years and Carlisle fans were angry that their club was now scrapping for survival with Scarborough. If you were looking for someone to blame, and the supporters certainly were, the evidence pointed to one man – Michael Knighton.

Knighton made his money in the 1980s property boom, buying houses and selling them at the right time. I'd first seen him in 1989 when he emerged from obscurity onto millions of television screens. Dressed in tracksuit top and shorts, he juggled a football and blasted it into the net at Old Trafford's Stretford End. Knighton had just bought Manchester United. Except he hadn't. All that bluster turned out to have little substance.

Knighton's face was all over the papers for a few weeks, then his backers withdrew. The deal was off. Knighton claimed to have pulled out in protest at the media coverage, which seemed strange for a man so obviously in love with the spotlight. He settled for a seat on the board. He had almost bought the biggest football club in the world for £10 million. It would have been the bargain of the century.

After three years at Old Trafford, Knighton set his sights 120 miles up the M6 and ninety-one places down the League. In 1992 Carlisle finished bottom of the Fourth Division. They might have been relegated to the Conference if Aldershot hadn't gone bust midway through the season. Carlisle were in a mess. That's why Knighton went there. He would turn them around and show a sceptical world that he wasn't just a bullshitter who couldn't deliver. He promised Premier League football in ten years. Seven years down the line, Carlisle were nearer the Northern Premier League. In the early 1970s Cumbria had three Football League clubs. Workington and Barrow had fallen through the trapdoor, and were perfect examples of the obscurity waiting down there. Carlisle looked set to join them.

Still, Knighton's masterplan had started promisingly. Carlisle were promoted to Division Two, twice, but went straight back down both times because of a lack of investment in the team. Knighton sold the fruits of the youth policy, including Matt Jansen to Crystal Palace and Rory Delap to Derby County, for millions of pounds. None of the proceeds were spent on replacements. The national media was more interested in Knighton the ball-juggling flying-saucer spotter. In 1996 he claimed to have seen a UFO while driving on the motorway. An alien voice said to him, 'Michael, don't be afraid.' While the papers lapped it up, Carlisle's supporters squirmed.

The downward spiral really started in 1997 when Knighton sacked manager Mervyn Day six games into the season. Day had just taken the club into Division Two and won the Auto Windscreens Shield at Wembley. If his dismissal was bizarre, what followed was even more incredible: Michael Knighton decided the best person to be Carlisle United's manager was Michael Knighton.

The BBC's *Football Focus* ran a feature showing Knighton the chairman in conversation with Knighton the coach. Midway through the season both Knightons emigrated to the Isle of Man and faxed instructions to the team. Knighton took over as coach of a Division Two side with massive potential. When he stepped down a year later, the best players had been sold and Carlisle were four places from the bottom of Division Three. At Christmas 1998 Nigel Pearson was appointed as manager. Nigel had been a great player for Middlesbrough but he had no managerial experience. He was thrown in at the deep end. We all were.

The fans' anger towards Knighton was affecting the team. Sometimes anger can unite people, but I didn't get that feeling at Carlisle. The players were low. Most of them were young and their careers were at stake. They had been battered by bad results and by Knighton dismantling the squad. On transfer deadline day, a few weeks before I arrived, Knighton had sold Tony Caig, Carlisle's only fit goalkeeper, to Blackpool for just £5,000. The fans were in uproar. How hard was the chairman trying to keep his club in the Football League? There were rumours that Knighton wanted to take Carlisle into the Scottish League. Fans were worried about what sort of future, if any, their club would have if it was relegated.

Tony Caig hadn't missed a game for three years; his replacement was Richard Knight, a nineteen-year-old loan signing from Derby County who had never played a League match. Knight played six times for Carlisle and was set to finish the season there. Then Derby's first-choice goalkeeper, Russell Hoult, was sent off. While he was suspended Derby played Mart Poom in goal. They needed a goalkeeper on the bench, so they recalled Richard Knight. For the last three games of the season

Carlisle were up the creek without a 'keeper. And that's where I came in. I walked in and I was fresh. That's what Nigel Pearson wanted, someone to say, 'Come on, lads, it's not a problem.' Even if it was.

Seven minutes into my Carlisle debut, on 24 April, I was picking the ball out of the net: Carlisle 0, Darlington 1. It was a deflected shot that completely wrong-footed me – just what I needed. Carlisle didn't look confident but goals by strikers Scott Dobie and Richard Tracey gave us a 2-1 half-time lead. We conceded two more before Ian Stevens grabbed the equaliser: 3-3. It was a point we didn't have before the game and we were grateful for it. Scarborough lost at home to Cardiff. We were four points ahead with two games left. Scarborough still had a game in hand. I drove home to my parents and came back up on Tuesday night.

The following Saturday we were at Hartlepool. I'd never played there before and I'd never played against Peter Beardsley. He was finishing his career at Hartlepool, a career that had started at Carlisle twenty years earlier. If Beardsley was feeling sentimental, he didn't show it. He showed a few glimpses of his ability, and so did I. We drew 0-0 and I was named Man of the Match. The point was enough to guarantee Hartlepool's survival. We looked on as their players and fans celebrated at the final whistle.

The draw should have been a good result for us too. But we got into the dressing room to hear that Scarborough had won at Halifax. Scarborough were now just two points behind us and they had two games to play. We had only one game left. Our fate was no longer in our own hands. I drove home again. My parents were already nervous about next Saturday. They weren't the only ones.

On Tuesday I returned to Carlisle. The following night Scarborough played their game in hand, at home to Plymouth, and won 3-0. They moved one point ahead of Carlisle, who were now bottom of the Football League for the first time all season. If Scarborough won their last match, at home to Peterborough, Carlisle would be relegated. The only way we could survive was by winning our home game against Plymouth and hoping Scarborough drew or lost.

The tension during the next few days was crippling. A lot of the players were scared. I could feel it everywhere in the club. Everyone in Carlisle was apprehensive. They just wanted Saturday's game to be over.

Everywhere I went, people were saying, 'You've got to win!' They meant well, but it didn't help. Having been in football for ten years, I knew it wasn't that simple. Even the best team in the world loses sometimes, and Carlisle were far from that.

The day before the big match Nigel Pearson took me into his office. 'I'm not going to tell the young lads who's playing tomorrow,' he said. 'I don't think it would do them any good.'

We trained, then had a five-a-side match. I played up front. I charged around like a maniac and scored a hat-trick, including the winning goal with a penalty. I was very vocal and dominant. It was my attempt to lift the lads, to try and get a bit of emotion into them, because I knew that's what they needed the following day. If they froze or panicked they were finished. I was scared myself but I could hide it better than most.

After training I had lunch with a couple of the lads. Everyone was well aware of the situation but players don't talk about stuff like that. Even with so much at stake, no one admitted they were frightened. Maybe they thought it would be a sign of weakness. Back at the hotel I went for a stretch in the gym, which I'd never done before. I was trying to do the right things because I couldn't afford to make a mistake next day.

The *Cumberland News* that Friday had two main stories. One was about Carlisle United's newly published accounts. The club had just announced a record profit of £1.4 million. Only Manchester United, Arsenal, Chelsea, Newcastle and Aston Villa had made more money. 'Most companies in Carlisle would give their left arm for results like these,' said Michael Knighton, who owned ninety-three per cent of the shares. The other story reported that Cumbria Police had rejected Knighton's request for protection the following afternoon. He claimed his children had been verbally abused and his wife was scared to go out. Carlisle United had become a family business: Michael Knighton's wife was marketing director, his son was publications co-ordinator and his daughter was a receptionist at the club.

Claudia was working in Nottingham that night. We spoke on the phone. Our relationship was in big trouble. Neither of us knew where our careers were heading. We were both insecure and we had become bad for each other. A couple of weeks before coming to Carlisle I'd met Sasha, my first girlfriend, in London. I hadn't seen her for ten years. She gave me her phone number and I talked to her every day in Carlisle. We were getting on really well. On the eve of the biggest game of my life, I was confusing things even more.

★

If you liken our club reception to a tree, the vultures are bending the branches to breaking point and the scavenging seagulls and voluminous vultures are waiting to give Michael Knighton the bird. If we lose on Saturday, I will be the sacrificial lamb and my head will be on the staffpike [sic] at the head of Brunton Park because that is the Roman-Christian culture and the lion's den that the media, the silent majority and the not-so-silent minority have created for us all.
Michael Knighton, On The Ball, ITV, Saturday, 8 May 1999

I woke on Saturday morning white as a ghost. I had some beans on toast and tried to focus my mind. Nigel had told us to wear our tracksuits instead of our suits and to get to the ground earlier than usual, about one o'clock, so he could run through the set-pieces. When I arrived at Brunton Park a little girl stopped me. She said, 'Before he left, Tony Caig said I could have his shirt. Can I have yours instead?'

'No worries. Find me after the match.'

The atmosphere was uneasy. Throughout the day it felt like we were on autopilot. It felt like it had all been pre-planned and we were acting out a show, just waiting until the final whistle to find out what the outcome was. We got changed and did the same things as usual. No one talked about what would happen if we lost. No one talked about what would happen if we won. No one talked about anything.

We warmed up. The ground was getting fuller. Back in the dressing room Nigel gave his team talk. One of the coaches was handing a bottle of brandy to anyone who wanted to try and calm their nerves. A couple of players took a swig. Normally I'd say that was unbelievable, but nothing surprised me about that day.

So here we were. This bunch of young men, average age twenty-four, had the task of keeping the Football League status Carlisle had held since 1928. My trip to Carlisle – the chance to rebuild my confidence – had come down to this.

At five to three we ran out. Brunton Park was packed. As the game kicked-off I tried not to think of the consequences of winning or losing, tried not to think, 'If I drop this cross...' In the first minute I came for the first corner, caught it and half-volleyed the ball the length of the field into the path of Ian Stevens. I settled down a bit then, but I still didn't want the ball coming anywhere near my goal.

After seven minutes there was a huge roar from the crowd: Peterborough had taken the lead at Scarborough. A couple of minutes later, Richard Tracey headed towards Plymouth's goal. The ball flicked off the crossbar. Ten minutes after that Scott Dobie powered in a header: GOAL! No – the referee disallowed it. It looked like being one of those days. We couldn't afford that. Not today.

Carlisle had been playing reasonably well but the disallowed goal kicked the fight out of us. On the plus side, Plymouth didn't seem up for it. It was easy to see how Scarborough had hammered them three days earlier. But Plymouth's indifference changed shortly before half-time. Their left-back, Paul Gibbs, went for a tackle with Carlisle's Tony Hopper. The crack of Gibbs' leg was heard around the ground. The game was held up for five minutes while he was treated and stretchered off. It was accidental but it fired Plymouth up and they came at us like a pack of wolves. Their Carlisle-born midfielder Steve McCall was running the show for them, spraying perfect passes all over the pitch. It must have been a difficult afternoon for him.

As we entered first-half stoppage time there were groans all around Brunton Park: Scarborough had equalised. At half-time some of the players couldn't keep still. Scott Dobie paced up and down in the shower room. Nigel Pearson's team talk was delivered with more urgency. 'We have to win this game,' he said. 'We HAVE to win! You've got forty-five minutes. This is your destiny.'

Two minutes into the second half Steve McCall passed the ball to Lee Phillips in Plymouth's half. Phillips ran it down the line and cut inside onto his left foot. No one tackled him. He unleashed a low shot which skidded past my right hand into the corner of the goal. The stadium was silent, except for the cheers of the Plymouth fans in the far corner. I ran to the goal, picked the ball out and punted it to the centre circle. We needed to score two goals now. We'd been struggling to score one.

'That's it,' I thought. 'We're down'.

The crowd started turning on Michael Knighton. Chants of 'Fat, greedy bastard!' battered Brunton Park. Years of anger and frustration were coming out. You'd expect the Carlisle players to be running their hearts out, running themselves into the ground, going down fighting.

Maybe they were, but they didn't seem to be. They were like ghosts floating through it. The fans wanted their team to steamroller Plymouth with a display of character and commitment. It wasn't there. I was thinking, 'Come on, fellas, this is your career! This is your life! What's wrong with you? I can go back to Swindon, but what are you going to do?'

With half an hour left I launched a clearance to Graham Anthony. He dribbled down the left side and hit a cross. The clearance fell at the feet of our captain, David Brightwell, twenty-five yards from goal. He ran onto it and lashed the ball into the net. The equaliser. A spark of life.

Precious minutes ebbed away. All around the ground you could feel the realisation that this was it. The fans were crying even as they were shouting. The Tannoy announcer was trying to get everyone going. I was aware of that without being aware of it; I could hear someone saying something, then the crowd would buzz a bit more and I could hear them shouting but couldn't make out the words. All my attention was focused on the ball and their goal, just willing the ball to go in their goal.

News filtered through to the fans behind me that Scarborough's game had ended. I could hear them yelling the final score: 1-1. Our destiny was back in our hands. The fourth official held up the board to show four minutes of added time. The injury to Paul Gibbs had given us the advantage of finishing after Scarborough, but we still needed a goal. As the seconds ticked away, I kept launching the ball upfield, praying the next whistle wouldn't be the last. My thigh was burning with the effort of bombing the ball forward as quickly as possible.

We were well into added time when Scott Dobie hit a cross from the right. It came off a Plymouth defender and went out for a corner. I looked across at Nigel Pearson. At other times when I've wanted to run up the field, people have told me to go back. 'What are you doing? Stay where you are!' The same old mentality. No entertainment in them. No faith in football to come up with a wonder moment. But now I thought, 'Sod it.' What was there to lose? Absolutely nothing. This was it. If it had been an older manager or someone more cynical they would have told me to stay where I was, but Nigel shrugged his shoulders and waved me up.

I began my 100-yard dash up the pitch, hoping to arrive in the penalty area before Graham Anthony took the corner.

Nine

THE GREAT ESCAPE

The final whistle sounded at the McCain Stadium in Scarborough. Thousands of home fans poured onto the pitch and sang along as 'All Right Now' blared out from the speakers. Scarborough *v.* Peterborough had finished 1-1. So, they thought, had Carlisle *v.* Plymouth. It had been far too close for comfort, but Scarborough's twelve-year stay in the Football League was extended for at least another season.

In the home dressing room the champagne was on ice. On *Grandstand*, Steve Ryder stressed that Carlisle and Plymouth were still playing.

There was no such caution in the boardroom. Scarborough's directors were about to uncork a bottle of bubbly. The chairman's wife watched the fans dancing on the pitch. Then she saw the dancing stop. A friend of the chairman was getting commentary from the Carlisle game on his mobile. He dropped the phone.

I arrived in Plymouth's penalty area as Graham Anthony's corner floated over from the right. No one marked me because no one saw me coming. I ran towards the ball, realised I wouldn't get the header, and kept going for the six-yard box. Scott Dobie thumped in a near-post header. The goalkeeper parried it. The ball dropped at my feet. I steadied myself and lashed out with my right foot. The ball flew hard and low into the net.

There was a split second of stunned silence, then an enormous roar. I raised my arm and turned in celebration. Before I could run, my teammates threw themselves at me and dragged me to the ground. Thousands of fans poured onto the pitch. I was entwined with David Brightwell under a pile of players.

'Brights – I think I've just scored the winner!'

'Yeah,' he said, 'but we're getting fucking squashed!'

91

Fans were hurling themselves onto the mountain of bodies. Brights grabbed my head. We couldn't breathe. We were screaming: 'Get off! GET OFF!'

After what felt like forever, they did. I staggered to my feet. Hundreds of people were lunging at me, hugging and kissing me. Fans were swinging on the crossbar. I was shouting, 'Get off the pitch! The game isn't over!' I thought we still had a couple of minutes to play. I thought Plymouth would break and I'd have to save it. I was shaking to my bones with adrenaline. I ran back down the pitch as people mauled me. My nose was pissing blood. I must have been kneed in the face while I was on the ground. My gloves were covered in blood. I looked for my towel in the goal. Someone had nicked it. I composed myself and steadied my breathing: okay, everyone's off the pitch, calm down, concentrate on the game...

I didn't see Plymouth's goalkeeper standing in the centre circle. If I'd looked up I would have realised there was no time left, and I would have been standing next to him. But I was on my goal line, as far from the tunnel as I could get. Plymouth kicked off. The referee blew the final whistle. My goal had come with one second to spare.

The whistle was a starting pistol for the fans. I ran for the tunnel with my arms outstretched, screaming in elation. A sea of bodies hit me from all sides. They hoisted me up and carried me across the pitch. People were ripping at my gloves and shorts. Some were panicking and shouting, 'Let him through!' At the edge of the pitch they let me down and I groped my way through the crowd. As I broke through to the mouth of the tunnel, another surge of adrenaline hit me. I let out a war cry, screaming, 'Come on! COME ON!' I ran up the tunnel into a mass of television crews. The words tumbled out.

'I just kept my head down and hit it. I thought I was gonna balloon it over the bar to be honest with you but I couldn't miss from that distance. If Schmeichel can do it I can do it! I don't know, you just try your luck. Never pick up the goalie, do they?'

In the dressing room I was mobbed. Everyone was hugging every-one else. Someone tipped a bucket of orange juice over me. People were jumping on me and screaming congratulations. Nigel Pearson had his shirt off. He embraced a couple of people then he turned around and gave me the biggest hug. He was crying. A journalist gave me his mobile phone and the television crews filmed as I rang home.

'Hello, mum. I've just scored the winner.'

'Yes, darling, we know.'

We were bundled out along the corridor and up the steps to the directors' box. That's what you do at the end of every season, although this one had turned out to be a bit different. Everyone pushed me to the front. Thousands of fans had gathered on the pitch. They were cheering and chanting, 'Hero! Hero!' Someone said, 'Throw your shirt in!' I ripped it off and threw it into the crowd where it disappeared in a mad scramble. I regretted it later because I'd promised it to the little girl before the game, not knowing 10,000 people would be screaming for it. Nigel Pearson made a speech. He thanked the players, the directors and the fans for their support. He didn't mention the chairman.

We trooped downstairs. I was knackered. The adrenaline had drained me. I sat in the shower room, alone with my thoughts, until the television crews returned. Michael Knighton, the Fat Controller, was with them. I'd hardly seen him before. He planted a kiss on my forehead. He stank of cigar smoke. 'If that's not entertainment,' he said, 'I'm a banana.' He was all over me, then he got up and followed the cameras.

There was no escape from the noise so I went down the corridor into the physio's room. A couple of players were there trying to get away from the pandemonium. I sat on a bed for a while until it had died down. Everyone started to realise what a close shave it had been.

Back in the dressing room someone said the newspaper journalists wanted to speak to me. They took me to the press box at the top of the stand where about thirty reporters were waiting. The big guns from the national papers were out in force. They had come to Brunton Park expecting a wake. They had been given something else, something none of them could have invented.

'Will you be back here next season, Jimmy?'

'Well, you never know what's going to happen.'

I mean, I'd just scored the winner for Christ's sake. In the directors' suite I was presented with the Man of the Match award. Champagne corks were popping. Hands grabbed me everywhere I turned. Fans were yelling so loudly and so hoarsely I could hardly make out the words. Everyone was staring at me with disbelieving eyes.

By the time I returned to the dressing room, it was empty. Most of the lads had got changed and disappeared. There were a couple still hanging around and I asked them what was happening. Everyone was going to Leonardo's restaurant later that evening. No one actually stayed and told me. I could have driven back home and nobody would have known.

I was getting showered and changed when a group of men walked in. They were about to play on the pitch in an end-of-season sponsors' match. They weren't Carlisle fans and they weren't paying me the slightest bit of attention. There was no one else about. The corridors were deserted. I put my tracksuit on and walked outside. Nobody was there. I don't know if I expected thousands of people to be waiting for me. I don't know what I expected, but life, it seemed, was straight back to normal. From being carried off the pitch and talking to every news-paper in the country, I was suddenly me again. What do I do now? Should I get something to eat? I'll get some petrol. And a Topic.

I drove back to the hotel. My mobile was overflowing with messages. Family and friends, even people I hadn't spoken to in months, were ringing. I wanted to be with my parents. I could imagine Dad watching the results on Sky and crapping himself, because he's not the best spectator. I had planned to drive to Nottingham and meet Claudia but I rang to tell her I was staying an extra night in Carlisle. She was upset. She probably thought, 'He's scored this goal now so he's not interested in me.' It wasn't like that. I just couldn't leave Carlisle. It was my night to go out and enjoy myself. I hadn't been out drinking with the lads since I'd been there. You couldn't really, running up to the showdown. It wouldn't have been fair on the fans.

I got a taxi to Leonardo's. The players were with their families. It was hard for everyone to take in what had happened. I felt out of sorts. I didn't really feel involved. I'd been there only twelve days in total and my loan had just ended. I was no longer a Carlisle player. Martin Wilkinson, the chief scout, pulled me aside. 'We want you to come back next year,' he said. 'We're really impressed with you. The chairman wants to have a chat.'

'OK, we'll talk about it.'

We had a drink in the bar upstairs. My chat with the chairman would have to wait because Michael Knighton wasn't there. His status as the most hated man in Cumbria meant he didn't get out much. Even after my goal, several thousand people would have happily strung him up. Everyone was slowly getting pissed. A couple of cigars were on the go. We went to Buskers nightclub next door. As soon as I walked in the place erupted. Everybody wanted to buy me a drink. Strange men were trying to kiss me. I felt very uncomfortable.

At one o'clock exhaustion hit me. I'd expected a storming night but I was dead on my feet. I slipped out by the back door, got a taxi to the hotel and went straight to bed.

Next morning I set off for Swindon. That afternoon they were at home to Barnsley in their last game of the season. We had planned to have a players' drink after the match and I'd arranged to meet Claudia that night. I still hadn't seen any papers or the television. While driving through different counties I listened to their local radio stations. One presenter said, 'Listen to this – this is fantastic!' He played a recording of a commentator. He was screaming, 'That is the most amazing goal I have ever seen!' It was only after hearing it two or three times that I realised he was talking about me. All the way down the country, in every county I passed through, I was news.

I arrived at Swindon ten minutes before the end of the game and walked up into the stand. Usually I would come out to watch the match and everyone would blank me. Today was different. The players in the stand stood up and applauded. The crowd started buzzing. Photographers turned away from the pitch and pointed their lenses at me. Suddenly the game didn't exist any more. The players clapped and smiled and giggled among themselves. It probably didn't shock them that I'd gone and scored a goal. Most of them thought I was a nutter anyway. They knew I'd always fancied myself as a forward.

The game finished – Swindon lost – and I went downstairs with the lads. Swindon had stayed up by three points. We were standing outside the dressing room waiting for Jimmy Quinn to finish his bollocking, sorry, team talk. A couple of players dared me to go in. I opened the door and walked into the middle of the room. I didn't say a word, I just stood there. Everyone had been sitting in silence, then they looked up at me. Jimmy Quinn started laughing. Mike Walsh said, 'I don't believe you!' and started laughing. Everyone was pissing themselves. It was actually an enjoyable moment. For the only time at Swindon, everyone was with me. People were shaking their heads and chuckling. 'Only you,' they were saying. 'Only you could do that.' We went for a drink. It was Brian Burrows' leaving do, and Steve McMahon was there. He didn't know what to say to me. No one did. They couldn't put what had happened into words. I stayed for a few hours then went back to the house and saw Claudia. We didn't talk much either.

Television companies and newspapers were ringing my mobile constantly. I arranged to go on *GMTV* next morning. A cab picked me up at five o'clock to take me to ITV's Bristol studio. They plugged me into a monitor and asked me about the goal. I could hardly keep my eyes open. When I got home Sky rang. They wanted me at their London studio at twelve. On the way I popped into the club. Jimmy Quinn wanted to see me. Mike Walsh was with him – Quinny could never see anyone by himself. 'You've done really well for yourself, scoring that goal,' he said. 'You've got a lot of good publicity. If you get a better offer you can leave on a free transfer.' It wasn't quite what I wanted to hear. I thought the goal would set me up. Less than two days after scoring it my manager was inviting me to leave. Although I wasn't enjoying my time at Swindon, I thought it could change. I just needed a run in the team. Frank Talia hadn't played that well the previous season. I was on good money and they were still in the First Division. A month earlier Quinn had told me that I didn't inspire him. I looked at him and thought, 'What do I need to do to inspire you then, Jim?'

I took Claudia to Sky, where Kirsty Gallacher interviewed me. My goal was the main talking point of the day. It was the first time I'd actually seen it. It was also the first time I'd seen what happened at Scarborough, which had hardly crossed my mind until then. When I arrived at Sky the car-park attendant was watching the scenes from Scarborough on a television in his hut. I looked at the thousands of people on the pitch and thought, 'They were all really happy, and now they're really unhappy. And it's because of me.' I've felt guilty about that ever since.

Claudia and me were in the Hard Rock Café when my mobile rang yet again. The *Daily Mirror* wanted me at their newsroom. The editor, Piers Morgan, came charging out of his office to meet me. People were shaking my hand. They wanted me to do some really stupid things for their article. I was the 'Miracle Man' because I had performed 'The Miracle of Brunton Park'. I had to persuade Home Secretary Jack Straw to give Mohammed al Fayed a British passport, and I made Caprice fancy Robin Cook. It was a total piss-take but I didn't give a monkey's. The *Mirror* agreed to give £500 to the music club my brother Iain attends. I was embarrassed to ask them for it, which shows how naïve I was; when the *Mirror* rang, most people would have said, 'How much are you offering?'

1 At the age of fourteen I was part of the all-conquering Centre 21, the kings of West Surrey Boys' League. That's me in the grey vest, about to hit the hard stuff. Well, Pomagne.

2 My first Crystal Palace official photo, from 1989 when I'd just started my YTS apprenticeship. My hairstyle was very fashionable at the time…

3 Playing for Palace youth team during the 1991/92 season. I'm wearing a support over my injured right wrist, before anyone realised it was broken.

4 The Crystal Palace youth team squad that reached the 1992 FA Youth Cup final. Within a year, most of the class of '92 had been thrown out of football.

5 The Glass family: me, my brother Iain, my mum Sheila, dad Frank and brother Paul.

6 In 1989 Nigel Martyn signed for Crystal Palace –
and my path to the first team was blocked by
Britain's first £1 million goalkeeper.

7 Steve Coppell was Palace manager during my first
five years at the club. Steve is living proof that nice
guys can succeed in football.

8 Alan Smith replaced Steve Coppell as Palace boss. Alan is pictured with the Division One Championship trophy after taking Palace back into the Premier League in 1994.

9 Ron Noades bought Palace in 1981 and stayed at Selhurst Park for nearly twenty years. There were plenty of ups and downs along the way.

10 From left to right: Palace coaches Steve Harrison and David Kemp, chairman Ron Noades and manager Alan Smith. David Kemp went on to be my manager at Oxford, and Ron Noades had a spell as manager of Brentford when I played for them.

11 Striker Ian Wright was the driving force behind Palace's success in the late 1980s and early '90s. A superb player, but we didn't always see eye to eye.

12 *Above left:* Mel Machin signed me for Bournemouth in 1996. I don't recall being offered any of his champagne. (*Bournemouth Daily Echo*)

13 *Above right:* In 1997 Bournemouth became Europe's first community-owned football club. Trevor Watkins was chairman. (*Bournemouth Daily Echo*)

14 Sunday 19 April 1998: I had the honour of playing in Bournemouth's first match at Wembley. A great experience, although being credited with an own goal put a dampener on it. (*Bournemouth Daily Echo*)

15 In the summer of 1998 I signed a four-year contract with Division One club Swindon Town, watched by manager Steve McMahon. What could possibly go wrong? (*Swindon Evening Advertiser*)

16 Steve McMahon had been a great player for Liverpool and England, but managing Swindon proved a difficult job for him. (*Swindon Evening Advertiser*)

17 A rare sight – me playing for Swindon. I made just twelve first-team appearances in a year and a half at the County Ground. (*Swindon Evening Advertiser*)

18 Jimmy Quinn took over from Steve McMahon as Swindon manager. I think Quinny liked me about as much as I liked him. (*Swindon Evening Advertiser*)

19 *Above:* Saturday 8 May 1999, 4.55 p.m. – a little bit of history. (Picture by Phil Rigby/Cumbrian Newspapers Ltd)

20 *Opposite:* After scoring the goal that kept Carlisle in the Football League I would have liked to do a few cartwheels and run into the crowd like Pat Cash at Wimbledon – but my teammates had other ideas. I'm on the ground as they jump on me, and we're about to be joined by hundreds of fans. (Picture by Phil Rigby/Cumbrian Newspapers Ltd)

21 'Some people are on the pitch…' Carlisle fans celebrate on the hallowed turf of Brunton Park. (Picture by Phil Rigby/Cumbrian Newspapers Ltd)

22 Carlisle chairman Michael Knighton gives me a cigar-scented kiss, but his gratitude didn't last long. (Picture by Loftus Brown/Cumbrian Newspapers Ltd)

23 and 24 Every action has an equal and opposite reaction. Joy in Carlisle meant despair in Scarborough. (*Scarborough Evening News*)

25 Scarborough chairman John Russell fell into depression after my goal sent his club crashing out of the League. (*Scarborough Evening News*)

26 Stephen Brown, an unemployed waiter, takes charge at Brunton Park, January 2001. Just another day in the weird world of Carlisle United Football Club. (Picture by Jonathan Becker/Cumbrian Newspapers Ltd)

27 Me and Louise in Ayia Napa, Cyprus, June 1999, just a few days after we met.

28 In 2001 I walked away from football and became an IT salesman in Dorset. (Picture courtesy of BBC *Inside Out*)

29 With my beautiful family: my wife Louise and our twins Ella and Jack.

In the *Mirror* that day my goal was plastered across two pages; as the Miracle Man I had another two pages the next day. I looked out over Canary Wharf and felt like a star.

That afternoon I went to my parents' house. Dad had spent most of the Plymouth game hiding upstairs but he'd come down for the last few minutes. When they announced that I'd scored, he leapt out of his seat and ran around the house. Iain didn't understand what had happened but he recognised me on television. The local newsagent had collected all the Sunday papers and put them in a huge bundle for Mum. I read them and watched the video Mum had compiled. My goal had made the headlines of every Saturday-night news programme. On *Match of the Day* I was the first Football League player to be mentioned since the creation of the Premier League. Des Lynam said they had thought about naming me Man of the Day, 'But we deal with the Premier League here.'

It was interesting to compare what I'd said to the press with what I was reading now. After the match a journalist had asked me, 'Are you staying in Carlisle tonight?' and I'd replied, 'I don't know. I'll probably go back and find my car keys have been nicked!' According to the *Mirror*, I'd said, 'The lads nicked my car keys and they told me I wouldn't get them back until Sunday.' The lads must have thought I was a right prat. But I forgave the *Mirror* when they referred to my goal as 'the greatest escape of all time'.

Not everyone was caught up in the euphoria. Scarborough lodged a protest with the Football League against their relegation, arguing that Carlisle shouldn't have been allowed to sign me after the transfer deadline. The League pointed out that Scarborough, along with every other Football League club, had voted for a rule change the previous summer to allow clubs with no 'keeper to sign one after the deadline. It hadn't been allowed for the past few years. Scarborough felt Carlisle's problems were self-inflicted because they had sold Tony Caig without securing a permanent replacement. They had a point, but their appeal was rejected.

Scarborough's chairman John Russell said, 'I am just devastated. I don't know what to say. We have fought and struggled eighteen hours a day to keep this place going. To go out to a goal scored by a goalkeeper in the fourth minute of injury time, a goalkeeper who was signed after the deadline, is just too much to bear. This is a lovely club with lovely people and they have all given everything. It is just sad, sad, sad.'

Michael Knighton is one football chairman who has never said 'I don't know what to say.' On the contrary, he couldn't shut up. 'I believe in the hand of God. He had a little wink at me in the ninetieth minute and I thank Him very much. I believe in a Methuselah, Frankenstein, alien beings and flying saucers. But most of all I believe in on-loan goalkeepers from Swindon who score goals in the dying seconds.' Knighton also said, 'We'll never let this happen again.' Like I said, you can't believe everything you read in the papers.

I drove back to Swindon with Claudia. Next morning we started arguing. After two years, we ended our relationship there and then. I'd been close to the door a few times but this time I went through it. Talking to Sasha over the previous few weeks had helped give me the confidence to finish with Claudia. I never ended a relationship without having another to go into, which isn't something I'm particularly proud of.

In my car the mobile wouldn't stop ringing. It was one journalist after another. I switched it off and tried to think. I didn't want to go to my parents where everyone was happy while I was angry and miserable. I couldn't go back to the house I'd just made a dramatic exit from. So I did what any right-minded person would do: I drove to Belgium.

On the M25 I saw a sign for Dover. I drove there and straight onto a Calais ferry. There was a casino in Calais but it was closed, which was just as well. Quickly realising Calais is a dump, I drove with no destination in mind past Dunkirk and into Belgium. Brussels was fifty miles away. Compared with the driving I'd been doing to Carlisle and back, fifty miles was a stroll around the block. I arrived at ten o'clock and booked into a hotel. Next morning I rang home.

'Hi, Dad. I'm in Belgium.'

'Okay... take your time, relax. See you in a couple of days.'

I got up late, went to the cinema, walked around, took some pictures, and wondered what the hell I was doing in Belgium. After three days I'd had enough. I drove off the ferry at Dover and switched my mobile on. By the time I got through all the messages I was on the M25 and my brain was radioactive. Carlisle United had called; Michael Knighton wanted to speak to me. Carlisle City Council had invited me to their mayor-making ceremony. More journalists had been on, including one from Australia. Every national newspaper wanted to do a feature.

'Who is this Jimmy Glass?'

Ten

BACK TO EARTH

On Sunday 16 May, eight days after my goal, I drove back to Carlisle with Dad for the city council's mayor-making ceremony the following morning. The council wanted the Plymouth match ball for their Millennium Gallery. No one knew where it was – it had gone missing in the aftermath of the goal – so I offered my boots instead. I'd bought them for £40 at Chivers Sports on my first day in Carlisle. A few weeks later I was handing them over to be cast in bronze. A statue of the right one, the Puma King SPA that scored the winner, is now on permanent display; the original is safely tucked away as a bit of security for my old age. There were press reports about the council making me a Freeman of the City. This would have allowed me to drive my sheep through Carlisle – a right which, sadly, has yet to be granted.

On the Monday afternoon I returned to Brunton Park to meet Michael Knighton. He was very chirpy. 'Thank you,' he said. 'You don't know what it means to us not to be relegated. We were really impressed with your performances. We want to take over your contract from Swindon and build a team around you.'

I went away to think about it. At first I hadn't wanted to move to Carlisle, to drop from the First Division to the Third. But I changed my mind. It would be a fresh start. And where better than the city where I was now a hero? My Swindon contract had three years left. I was going to be on £50,000 for 1999/2000, rising by £5,000 in each of the following two years. It was good money, but I had £25,000 of gambling debts. My agent was Clive Whitehead at the PFA. I asked Clive to tell Michael Knighton I wanted £800 a week and a £20,000 lump sum at the start of each year of my contract. It worked out at £1,200 a week before tax – slightly more than I was on at Swindon. Those numbers weren't set in stone. When you're negotiating, you start with the highest figure. With my family 300 miles away, travelling home would be a big expense. I didn't ask for any bonuses or relocation money.

Clive rang me: 'All Michael Knighton said was, "That's a bit rich. I'll get back to you."' To this day I'm still waiting. Jimmy Quinn didn't help. He had told me I could leave Swindon on a free transfer. He told Knighton he wanted £15,000 for me. Journalists were asking Knighton if Carlisle would sign me. He said, 'Jimmy Glass has to lower his wage demands,' as if I was asking for a fortune.

If I was motivated by money I wouldn't have driven to Belgium when every sports writer in Britain was desperate to speak to me. If I was motivated by money I would have named my price a few weeks earlier, when Carlisle didn't have a goalkeeper. I know £1,200 a week is a lot of money but it wouldn't have made me the club's top earner. After what I'd done I expected a bit of payback. I was a professional footballer who did something beyond the call of duty. It's disheartening to look at players who are earning huge sums of money for what they *might* do. I actually *did* something – something of great significance.

In the back of my mind I thought Michael Knighton might say, 'Go on, son. Buy yourself a nice car. Have a holiday.' I'd just saved him millions of pounds – maybe even his life. The papers had shown photos of Knighton surrounded by stewards as fans hurled abuse at him in the seconds before my goal. If I hadn't scored he would have been lucky to get out of Brunton Park in one piece.

The day before my goal Knighton announced a club-record profit. A few days later the club shop was selling Jimmy Glass goalie tops at £40 a throw, Plymouth match videos and 'Great Escape' T-shirts. Then there's the small matter of Football League status, valued by clubs like Rushden and Diamonds and Yeovil Town at millions of pounds. The money which Third Division clubs receive from the Football League, plus the difference in gate receipts and sponsorship between Division Three and the Conference, is more than £500,000 a season. And Michael Knighton was calling my request for a small pay rise 'a bit rich'. That's just insulting. That made me wonder if I'd done the right thing by keeping Carlisle in the League.

I couldn't help comparing Knighton with John Russell, Scarborough's chairman. I didn't know him but he looked like someone who cared about his club, someone who had invested a lot of his life in Scarborough. I watched him on television, weeping with his head in his hands because I'd just kicked them out of the Football League. Then I thought about another chairman, the one who was laughing at Carlisle's fans and players, and then laughing at me.

The only money I ever made from the goal was a few hundred quid for appearances on Sky; I didn't even get a goal bonus from Carlisle because there wasn't one in my contract. When I had made the PFA my agents a few months earlier it never crossed my mind that I would have the opportunities that in fact came along. I should have had someone guiding me after the goal but that's not one of the PFA's strong points. They were just concerned with whether Carlisle would do a deal for me. It was a missed opportunity, but there were plenty of those.

Carlisle signed another goalkeeper, Luke Weaver, from Sunderland. He had just turned twenty and had played only fifteen League games. Carlisle paid him £1,000 a week.

I wasn't the only one to say goodbye to Brunton Park that summer. Nigel Pearson's contract was not renewed. Nigel's replacement was Keith Mincher, whoever he may have been. Mincher lasted less than a week before walking out, never to be seen again. Martin Wilkinson took over. He had been chief scout when I was there. Martin was a nice man but he didn't seem cut out for management. One of the few people who didn't leave the club was Michael Knighton; he remained still stubbornly clinging on.

In hindsight I'm pleased I didn't sign for Carlisle. It would have been very difficult for me to sit back and keep quiet about what Knighton was doing to the club. And if I had gone there my achievement would have been marred. That was the feeling among the fans as well. On the internet, people were saying, 'What's Jimmy Glass like as a goalkeeper? If he comes back, we might find out he's not that good.' I left Carlisle with a better record than many strikers – played three, scored one. I rode into town, saved the football club, and rode out. Perfect.

I went to Ayia Napa in Cyprus for a friend's stag week and told Sasha we'd sort things out when I got back. We'd seen each other a couple of times but Sasha didn't want us to rush into a relationship in case I met someone in Cyprus. Loads of people recognised me in Ayia Napa. I met Rio Ferdinand and Frank Lampard out there. I knew Rio because he'd been on loan at Bournemouth from West Ham a couple of years earlier. All he wanted to talk about was my goal. Rio's friend handed him a camera and asked Rio to take a picture of me and him. I laugh about that now but at the time I probably took it too seriously. I thought I was a superstar. I hadn't been playing that well and I wasn't super-fit, but that summer I was top dog. The adulation that came my way gave me a false sense of security. I thought I was better than I really was.

On the beach I met Louise. I tried to impress her by doing a bungee jump, which didn't work because it turned out she'd already done ten of them. We sat up and talked all night. Louise is from Bournemouth. I told her I used to play for Bournemouth but she'd never heard of me. She had a boyfriend but I got the feeling her heart wasn't in it. I told her the world was at her feet and she could do anything she wanted. That's how I felt. If it wasn't for the goal I would never have had the confidence to try and attract someone like Lou. She was so beautiful, in her looks and her personality. She had a sparkle in her eye and a belief in life.

Ayia Napa was a footballers' playground. Southampton striker James Beattie was there, looking very much as if he was trying to pull Louise. She had met him before and she told me he had a Porsche, which made me very jealous. But Lou and I were getting on really well. Now all I had to do was tell Sasha. Her feeling that I might meet someone else had proved right.

In July I returned to Swindon for pre-season training. And I brought a question with me: how the hell do I follow that? I was still only twenty-five, which is a bit young to have the rest of your life as an anticlimax. The feeling was cushioned by a huge pile of letters. There were hundreds of them, many from Carlisle fans but also from football supporters in general who had been overwhelmed by the goal, from all over Britain and all around the world.

Dear Jimmy,
Here's a tenner. Get yourself a couple of pints and a box of chocolates for your mum.
*   If I live to be a thousand I'll never ever witness anything like that again and I hope to God I never do!*

Dear Jimmy,
Congratulations on your fantastic and unique achievement. Best wishes for
your future success, in goal or out of goal!
Gordon Taylor, PFA chief executive

The most astonishing event I have ever seen.

In over 30 years of supporting Carlisle United I have seen us top of the First
Division, win at Wembley, a League Cup semi-final, and an FA Cup quarter-
final. Nothing, however, will ever match sitting in a hotel lobby in Kuwait in
floods of tears as my mother told me over the telephone that you had scored for
us to save our skins. Please stay, Jimmy. You are now regarded as GOD.

The media fascination continued too. The *Carlisle News & Star*
produced the 'Jimmy glass', a pint pot featuring my head topped with a
crown and the words 'Jimmy Rules!' They also produced an 'I Was
There' T-shirt, and together these items raised £1,000 for Mencap.
BBC Radio Five made a series which looked at great sporting come-
backs. The first programme was about that afternoon at Brunton Park.
It contrasted the events and emotions at Carlisle and Scarborough. It
was strange to hear Scarborough's chairman, manager and players
describing their feelings when they heard I'd scored. *The Rough Guide*
to English Football featured me on its cover. *Total Football* magazine
published a list of the 100 most bizarre events in football history. My
goal was number three, beaten only by Eric Cantona's karate kick and
Glenn Hoddle's opinions about disabled people. Jeremy Paxman asked
a question about my goal on *University Challenge* – they knew the
answer – and it cropped up again on *A Question of Sport*. 'What
happened next?' asked Sue Barker as I arrived in Plymouth's penalty
area. You'd have needed to have spent the summer on Mars not to
know. Ally McCoist pointed out the referee's fate in the moments after
the goal. As I lay trapped on the ground, a Carlisle fan sprinted onto
the pitch, leapt over the pile of bodies and embraced the ref in a bear
hug. The ref fell over, then staggered to his feet, just in time to be
knocked down again by a fan coming from the other direction.

In the papers Alex Ferguson said my goal was amazing. I was invited
to a charity golf day where George Graham asked to be introduced to
me. George was the Tottenham manager at the time so I jumped at the

chance. I thought, 'Great – he wants to offer me a contract!' but he just wanted to offer his congratulations.

A headline in *The Times* summed it all up for me: 'Glass Crystallises the Beauty of the Game'. In the article I said that the publicity surrounding the goal wasn't really about me. It was about the fact that in the world of £50,000-a-week wages and David Beckham's hair, something could happen to make people step back and realise why they love football. There was no 'Sponsored by Barclaycard', no hype or glamour. I scored in front of a ramshackle terrace at the bottom of Division Three, but the passion which my goal generated spread much further. There are ninety-two League clubs, but in many people's eyes there's only the Premiership. In a world where the Premiership is decided by who's got the most money and football has become predictable, my goal reminded fans everywhere why the game is so special. Football needs moments like that, now more than ever. Look at how the game has changed to safeguard the big clubs at the expense of excitement. These days the top clubs are handed so many chances to succeed that the thrill of seeing them fail is a distant memory. The Premiership winners go into the Champions League while the runners-up have to make do with – the Champions League. Third place? Champions League. And the club that limped into fourth place on goal difference? Champions League. Even clubs that are knocked out of the so-called Champions League have a UEFA Cup safety net.

In 2002/03, eight of the twenty Premiership sides qualified for Europe. When only the best team won, the rest had to get better. But now that so many back doors have been opened, everyone is looking for a way to sneak through. Fans have come to see success as their right. This expectation adds to the pressure on chairmen to hire and fire if managers don't succeed within a few months. It encourages short-term thinking – throwing money at one player instead of looking ahead and investing in youth.

Compare the changes at the top with those at the other end of the League ladder. In 2002/03 the situation for struggling League clubs became even worse when relegation for Division Three's bottom two was introduced. Of the last eight clubs to be relegated from the League only Doncaster have regained their former status, and it took them five years. If you want football as Bill Shankly's 'life and death', that's where you'll find it.

★

One thing my new-found fame didn't bring was offers of employment. Maybe it scared a few managers. They don't want their goalkeeper to be the centre of attention. Whatever the reason, I was looking down the barrel of reserve-team football again. Jimmy Quinn obviously wasn't thinking, 'Fantastic, you now inspire me.' I mentioned this to Mike Walsh. He told Quinny, who took me to one side. 'It's not that I don't want you here,' he said. 'It's just, if you get something else you can leave.'

Claudia and I sold our house in Swindon. I made about £7,000 on the deal, which disappeared into the black hole of my gambling debts. I didn't want to buy another house in Swindon because I didn't expect to be there for much longer. I drove in every day from London or Bournemouth, where Louise lived.

The season started with Frank Talia in goal. While he was number one, my squad number was thirteen. Was somebody trying to tell me something? I was back playing for the reserves on Wednesday afternoons. Television crews and journalists were turning up to do reports about me. People's attitudes at Swindon began changing: 'Living off that goal again, are you?' My goal didn't mean a lot to the players. Most footballers are cynical about football. Maybe it's their way of keeping the game's emotional power at arm's length. Even Michael Knighton didn't seem bothered. I was reduced to sitting by the phone like a lovesick teenager, thinking, 'Is he going to ring?' My goal meant a lot to the media and the fans, but football's establishment was dragging me back down to earth.

Swindon had a new goalkeeping coach. John Granville had played for Trinidad & Tobago and Millwall in the 1980s. He's the only coach I've worked with that I felt really knew what he was doing. By this time I was twenty-six and had been a professional footballer for ten years. I spent that decade blagging it off natural ability, which is the only way to become a good player in the lower divisions. With John I finally realised how goalkeeping should be broken down. I'd always thought goalkeeping technique should involve being on your toes, moving forward to narrow the angle, and John confirmed that. But Swindon would only pay for him to come in one day a week. He charged £100. I clubbed together with Frank Talia and Swindon's two young keepers to pay for an extra day.

A few weeks into the season, Plymouth expressed an interest in signing me. Although they had seen what a good striker I was that day in Carlisle, they wanted me as a goalkeeper. I spoke to their manager but nothing came of it. A week later Jimmy Quinn called me into his office. 'Carlisle have been on the phone,' he said. 'Their 'keeper's injured. Do you fancy going up there on loan?' It was almost exactly the same thing he had said five months earlier but my response was very different. 'I don't think so,' I said. 'Michael Knighton treated me like a prat. I could never go back to Carlisle as long as he's there.' It was a hard decision. I was stuck in the reserves and Carlisle were the only club interested. I would have gone to any club in the country, except the one I saved.

Swindon hit another losing streak and were soon bottom of Division One. At the end of September, Frank Talia jarred his back in training. We were at home to Blackburn that night. I played, and did well in a 2-1 win. Frank had been struggling for form and I'd been looking good, thanks to John Granville, so Jimmy Quinn said he would give me a run in the team. The next game was Bolton at home. We lost 4-0. I didn't play particularly well or particularly badly; Swindon just fell apart. Then we had Stockport at home and drew 1-1. Their goal came after I miskicked the ball to one of their players in the centre circle. He smacked it back over my head and into the net. It was voted one of the best goals of the season on Sky Sports. But it was my fault. I made a mistake and was punished. All credit to Jimmy Quinn: he said I'd played well.

Next week we visited top-of-the-table Fulham. With five minutes left it was 0-0. Then they got a free-kick just outside the penalty area. I called for four men to stand in my defensive wall but only three came. The fourth player had been substituted and the lad sent on in his place hadn't been told that he had to be part of our walls. The ball was smashed through the gap where my player should have been. I saved it, but Fulham scored from the rebound and won the match. Jimmy Quinn wasn't happy with the wall. I asked him why our substitute hadn't been told to stand in the wall. 'That's not for us to think about,' he said. 'You've got to think for yourself on the pitch.'

That's one of the most ironic things I ever heard from a football manager. We lack players who can use initiative and take the game by the scruff of the neck because footballers have had self-expression bullied out of them by managers. Managers don't want leaders in the dressing room, but they expect them to suddenly appear on the pitch.

After Fulham, we lost 1-0 at Barnsley then had two home games: we won one and drew one. At Bolton the following Saturday, Swindon didn't have a shot on target. I made half a dozen good saves in wet conditions. With three minutes left Bolton's Bob Taylor hit a weak shot from the edge of the penalty area. I tried to get my chest behind it but the ball slid through my arms and trickled into the goal. We conceded another straight afterwards. As I trudged off the pitch after the final whistle one of my teammates came up to me. 'That was fucking awful, Jimmy,' he said. A Bolton fan shouted, 'Fuck off, Glass! You're shit!' I glared in his direction and made a 'wanker' sign. Then I glanced up at the Reebok Stadium's video screen, and saw a huge close-up of myself giving a 'three types of the finest coffee bean' gesture.

In the dressing room Jimmy Quinn started murmuring that he was embarrassed, there's no excuse, that's just crap. Suddenly the fact that we'd been battered for ninety minutes came down to me making one mistake. When you mess up as a goalkeeper, there's nowhere to hide. You apologise and hope your team will back you. I was looking for someone to say, 'Come on, boss. He kept us in the game.' It didn't happen. That was the dog-eat-dog mentality that Quinn had instilled. Instead of looking at the defence or the forwards as a unit, he blamed individuals. Managers do that because they're insecure. They want to keep everyone separate so they can't gang up on them. When Mel Machin did that at Bournemouth it united us. Machin created team spirit without realising it. We were united in the belief that he was a nutter. We were young lads and we stuck together. Swindon had more experienced, cynical pros. The consensus was, 'Don't get involved. Watch your own back.'

When you become a footballer you get sucked into that mentality: 'If I try and help someone but get out of position, I'm the one who'll get bollocked. That's my career in jeopardy. So I'll just do enough to cover my arse.' Players who care about the game feel powerless so they don't rock the boat. They take their money and get on with it. Maybe I could have kept my mouth shut and I'd be driving a Porsche by now. Maybe I should have.

Jimmy Quinn destroyed team spirit when he could have been using it to his advantage. He was looking for scapegoats because Swindon were bottom of the league. Swindon were struggling for various reasons. The main one was that the players weren't performing as a team. There were good individuals, like George Ndah, Iffy Onuora and Mark Walters, but they were badly organised.

On the coach back to Swindon from Bolton, Frank Talia's girlfriend rang him. Jimmy Quinn had slated us on the radio, me in particular. I saw it in the papers the next day: 'We had ten outfield players who ran their hearts out today, yet we lost the game and it's down to one individual. I was embarrassed for the fans. Good goalkeepers don't make mistakes like that.' It was one of the lowest points of my career, being personally attacked by someone who was supposed to protect me. If it's kept in-house you can knuckle down. But when a manager goes public, unless he's man enough to retract it your career at that club is over. Letters and phone calls from fans streamed in to Quinn and the *Swindon Evening Advertiser*. Some criticised me; others said, 'How can a manager treat his players like that?' I got letters saying 'Keep your head up.' The *Advertiser* printed an article headlined 'Who'd be a goalkeeper?'

Quinn recalled Frank Talia for the next match, at Huddersfield. Maybe I deserved to be dropped for my mistake at Bolton. Before the Huddersfield game Quinn apologised to the players for his anger the previous week. He never apologised to me. If he had I would have forgotten about it. People make mistakes, whether they're dropping the ball or saying the wrong thing. But he never had the balls to say sorry. He even tried to make a joke of it. He said, 'You were crap, though, weren't you?', not realising the damage he'd done, or not caring. Swindon lost 4-0 at Huddersfield. Swindon goalkeeper was a difficult position that year. I went back to the reserves. The first team's next win came four months and twenty matches later.

In November, Carlisle travelled to Dr Martens League side Ilkeston Town in the first round of the FA Cup, and lost. Carlisle were near the bottom of Division Three again. 'We'll never let this happen again.'

Eleven

OUT OF THE FRYING PAN

One Monday in November, Frank Talia picked up an injury and didn't train all week. On the Thursday I woke up in Bournemouth feeling ill with a sore throat so I didn't go in. Thursday was the players' day off. John Granville, the goalkeeper coach, was due in but I would still pay him and the two young 'keepers would be there. Next morning Jimmy Quinn asked where I'd been. I told him. He said, 'Frank's injured and you can't be bothered to come in and train with the 'keeper coach?'

'I was ill,' I replied, 'and it was the players' day off. Anyway, I'm paying for John out of my own pocket.'

He gave me a written warning, for not attending a training session I'd arranged myself and was paying for myself. If you get three written warnings you can be sacked. He sent me home for the weekend and said if I spoke to any journalists he would fine me.

After Jimmy Quinn said I didn't inspire him, I scored that goal. I might be remembered more for that than he is for his 300. Maybe that's why he took a dislike to me. After giving me a written warning he made me train with the youth team. 'You're not one of my players,' he said. 'I didn't sign you.' Lots of players who move into management are bitter that they're not still playing and that eighteen-year-olds are being paid more than they earned in their prime. They can't see past their glory days. All you hear is, 'I never did it like that when I was younger.' When Jimmy Quinn arrived at Swindon, he said, 'We're going back to the days of Lou Macari.' We were on the verge of a new millennium. The possibilities for mankind were infinite. And Jimmy Quinn wanted to go back to the days of Lou Macari.

One day Quinn said, 'Cambridge phoned a few weeks ago. They haven't been back in touch so they must have either watched you or rung Bournemouth and Bournemouth must have slated you,' which I could easily imagine Mel Machin doing. I rang Clive Whitehead at the PFA and asked him to get on to Cambridge. Their manager, Roy McFarland, had been impressed with me when Swindon reserves beat Cambridge reserves. Roy said he already had two goalkeepers and couldn't do anything until he offloaded one. I told him I should be able to get a free transfer and he asked me to keep him informed.

Swindon's financial problems were escalating. Mark Walters was allowed to leave because the club couldn't afford his wages. George Ndah, Iffy Onuora and Ty Gooden were sold. I said I would consider terminating my contract for a pay-off. We negotiated a £25,000 settlement to be paid in two instalments of £12,500. I owed £20,000, so that would clear my debts and leave me with £5,000 while I tried to rebuild my career. At the end of January 2000 I signed the forms, said goodbye to the office girls and left.

I could have stayed at Swindon and picked up £140,000 over the next three years for an easy life in the reserves. But it was more important to play first-team football.

Having negotiated this settlement, it was a surprise to read in the *Sun* and the *Daily Mail* that Swindon had sacked me. My dad made enquiries and discovered that the story had been supplied by Tony Ford, a freelance journalist who had criticised me at Bournemouth. Under the conditions of my contract termination Swindon couldn't comment, so Tony Ford had decided to send a press release around the papers saying I'd been fired. Players get fired for taking drugs or punching somebody, and here I was trying to find a job.

I rang the *Sun* to complain. They didn't retract their mistake but they ran a story which mentioned my 'netbusting antics' at Carlisle. Something which had been considered fantastic eight months earlier was now regarded as 'antics', as if saving a club with a seventy-one-year League history was some sort of comedy show. I rang Brendan Batson, who was deputy chief executive at the PFA. He sent letters to the *Sun* and the *Mail* but didn't get much response. Brendan said, 'You don't want to wind the papers up. Just forget about it.' I was livid. Dad wrote to the Press Complaints Commission and the papers eventually printed a correction.

The first half of my Swindon settlement was due. I rang the club's chief executive and he confirmed the money would be in my account that afternoon. It wasn't. Next morning I read in the paper that

Swindon had gone into administration the previous day. I'd just torn up a contract worth £140,000 for less than one-fifth of that amount, and now it seemed I wouldn't even get that. The PFA said they couldn't do anything until the club came out of administration.

I explained the situation to Roy McFarland at Cambridge and he gave me a month's contract for £500 a week. In footballing terms, Swindon to Cambridge was frying pan to fire – from the bottom of Division One to the bottom of Division Two. The Premiership clubs had just signed a new contract with Sky, which gave them £1.65 billion over the next three years, double the previous contract. Each Premiership club now received more than £20 million a year in television revenue alone. It didn't look as if much of this money was trickling down the divisions. Football's revolution had certainly bypassed Cambridge. In 1992 they had almost reached the Premiership. Eight years later, the top clubs were handed so much money that smaller clubs couldn't compete without crippling themselves. Survival was now the height of their ambition. Having come within a few points of joining Manchester United and Arsenal, Cambridge were now lagging behind local Sunday league teams. The club trained at a private sports complex. This had several excellent pitches but these were reserved for pub teams. All Cambridge United could afford was a sloping pitch covered in potholes.

The papers heard I was at Cambridge and they said I was looking for a contract. Roy McFarland wasn't pleased. He thought I was using Cambridge to get other clubs interested. He said, 'Your people have told the papers that you're here.' I thought, 'What people? If my agent remembers my name I'm doing well.'

I was confident of a run in the team. Shaun Marshall, Cambridge's twenty-one-year-old first-choice goalkeeper, wasn't playing particularly well. At least the club had a goalkeeping coach. Unfortunately he was the kit man, just like at Crystal Palace. I don't know what it is about kit men and goalkeeping. It's like having a postman being taught by a priest. Cambridge's version was a little Turkish chap. His coaching consisted of placing the ball six yards out and smashing it in the corner of the goal.

I played five reserve games and we won every one. After a month I asked Roy what was happening. He said he couldn't offload Arjan Van Heusden, the number-two goalkeeper, and so he couldn't afford to sign me. Roy probably wasn't sorry to see me go. My mind wasn't focused on football and I think he sensed that. Every morning I was setting off from my parents' house at seven o'clock for a two-and-a-half-hour drive. Every time Roy walked past I was thinking, 'Is he going to offer me a longer contract?' In those circumstances it was hard to be as good as I needed to be to impress him. Part of me was bitter that my career was going wrong just a few months after I'd made head-lines around the world. The young lads at Cambridge looked at me like I was something special, but I didn't feel that way.

For the first time since signing my YTS forms with Palace at the age of fifteen, I didn't have a club. At least at Swindon there was money coming in; now I didn't even have that. With no income there was no way of paying my debts. I had to come clean to my parents about my gambling. I didn't want to tell them. I didn't want them to think anything bad about me or worry about me. I just wanted to be a success and for them to enjoy it.

Although they knew I'd visited the casino at Bournemouth, the scale of my problem came as a shock. But they were there for me, as they always have been. Dad took out a loan for £20,000, which I agreed to repay when my Swindon money arrived. I used the loan to pay off my debts. But within a few months I had run up another £30,000 of gambling debts – on top of the £20,000 I now owed Dad. At that time in my life, having scored my goal, I was loved by more people than I could ever have imagined. And I'd never felt so alone.

Steve Coppell was back in the manager's chair at Crystal Palace. I rang Steve and he said I could train there. Some things had changed for the better in the four years since I'd left. The club had a new training ground just off the M25. It was a converted school which looked more like a stately home – a far cry from the shed I'd been used to. Steve said he couldn't offer me a contract because the club had financial prob-lems. Didn't they all? But Palace's problems were more spectacular than most. They had gone up to the Premiership in 1997 and back down in '98. Then Mark Goldberg had bought the club from Ron Noades.

Goldberg was a Palace fan who put his money where his mouth was. The deal to buy Palace was initially £30 million for everything. This became £22 million, but with Ron Noades still owning Selhurst Park. This wasn't Goldberg's only questionable business decision. He hired

Terry Venables, who took a slice of all transfer fees and bought in players on big contracts, many of whom didn't perform. Goldberg's money dried up, leading to the sale of the best players. Mediocre high earners couldn't be offloaded and Palace ended up in administration. In trying to bounce straight back to the Premiership, they almost lost everything.

Clive at the PFA was ringing around to try and find me a club. He spoke to Ian Atkins, Chester City's manager, and Ian asked me to play a reserve game. Chester were ninety-first in the Football League. The only club below them was Carlisle ('We'll never let this happen again'). Of all the clubs in all the world it would have to be the one having a relegation battle with Carlisle. It occurred to me that Ian Atkins might have been playing mind games with Carlisle, knowing the effect it would have on them if I went to their relegation rivals. I thought about going. Mum and Dad didn't think I should. They said it would tarnish my achievement. All I had was the fact that I'd saved Carlisle. Could I throw that away for the sake of playing a few matches?

But I was unemployed. I had no income and I owed a small fortune. Going to Chester would bring in money and it would be a chance to establish myself again. The clincher was the fixture list. In three weeks' time, Carlisle were playing at Chester in one of the season's final matches. My decision was made. I asked Clive to ring Ian Atkins and say thank you, but I would not be taking up his offer. There's no way in the world I could have run out into a stadium of Carlisle fans and tried to send their team out of the League.

On transfer deadline day at the end of March, Second Division side Brentford approached me. Their manager was Ron Noades, who had bought Brentford after selling Crystal Palace. I spoke to Brentford's chief scout, Johnny Griffin. He told me they were looking for a 'keeper for the following season, which sounded promising. As a west London club, Brentford would have been a great move for me. Jason Pearcey and my former Palace colleague Andy Woodman had been competing for the number one shirt. Johnny Griffin said they would send Andy Woodman on loan to Peterborough and take me until the end of the season. I thought, 'Great. Ron Noades wants to have a look at me with a view to a permanent move.' Then Johnny told me how much Ron was offering − £350 a week. I'd just ripped up an agreement at Swindon for three times that amount. On Brentford's wages it would take me more than three years to earn what Roy Keane was making in a week at Manchester United.

I didn't know what to do. I spoke to Steve Coppell and he advised me not to sign. But I had no money and not much choice. Then Steve said, 'Come to Palace and I'll give you £400 a week.' I'd have loved to go back there but Fraser Digby was doing really well in goal. I had a far better chance of first-team football at Brentford, so I signed for them and Andy Woodman went to Peterborough.

For Brentford's next game, at home to Wigan on 1 April, I was on the bench. Brentford were 1-0 down when Jason Pearcey was taken off with an injury. I replaced him. We lost 2-0. I did all right, but Brentford brought Andy Woodman straight back from Peterborough and played him in the next match. I realised Ron Noades never had any intention of playing me. He only got me there to save money. He'd sent Andy Woodman to Peterborough so they would pay his wages, which were a lot more than £350 a week. It turned out that Brentford already had a 'keeper lined up for the following season, a bloke from Iceland who they decided to sign after watching him on video. A few days after I'd signed for Brentford, Fraser Digby injured his knee and was out for the rest of the season. If I'd gone to Palace I would have played the last six matches. It was another turn left when I should have turned right, having been led up the garden path by Ron Noades.

Ron was good at looking after the pennies. While some Second Division players were earning £2,000 a week, he didn't want to pay more than £500. That would have been fine if he was developing young players, but he wasn't. The squad was full of cheap foreign imports. Ron had scrapped the reserves so I wasn't playing at all. Brentford shared Crystal Palace's training ground, and one of my only games for Brentford was when the two sides played each other in a practice match. I played the first half up front and the second half in goal.

Andy Woodman picked up a virus before Brentford's last game of the season, at home to Colchester. With Jason Pearcey still injured I was starting my first League game for six months, since my final match for Swindon. Some of the lads said, 'Imagine if you scored in the last game of the season again!' I asked Ron Noades if he would let me take any penalties. 'No,' he said. The Colchester match was a goalless draw. My mind kept wandering to a game elsewhere.

Carlisle went into the final day as one of three teams who could be relegated from the Football League. I couldn't believe they were in trouble again. If Carlisle won at Brighton they were guaranteed to stay up. They lost 1-0. That left Shrewsbury and Chester. Shrewsbury won and were safe. Chester only needed a point from their home game with Peterborough to survive and send Carlisle down. Chester lost 1-0. Carlisle had done it again, or rather Peterborough had. A year earlier my goal would have meant nothing if Peterborough hadn't held Scarborough to a draw.

Carlisle's second escape was as unlikely as their first. The crucial match had been Chester *v*. Carlisle in April. Carlisle won 1-0, with an injury-time goal after two of their players had been sent off. Carlisle finished with ten points fewer than the previous season. They stayed up because their goal difference was better than Chester's, by just two goals. If Carlisle had gone down a year earlier they would probably have struggled to survive in the Conference.

The Great Escape was followed by The Grateful Escape. My moment of glory still mattered.

Twelve

THE CURRY-HOUSE CONMAN

No one said much to me after my last game for Brentford. It was a bit different to the end of the previous season. Now, in the summer of 2000, I was unemployed. I went to Sky Sports to talk about the day's ups and downs, using my status as relegation expert. There was a lot of media interest in me around the anniversary of my goal. That lunchtime I had featured on ITV's football show *On The Ball*. Gabriel Clarke reported on how my life had changed since the goal. The studio pundits couldn't understand why I didn't have a club. Barry Venison said, 'It would be a shame if the game lost a character like Jimmy Glass.' I like to think he was right, but the game has lost a lot of characters and no one does anything about it.

Sky's *Soccer AM* team rang me live on air when they heard I was without a club. They told me to advertise myself to the nation. My personal ad should have gone something like this: 'Hi there. My name is James. I'm six foot four and have skilled hands, if you know what I mean. And I'm very good at keeping it up – Carlisle United, that is. I have plenty of experience but am always eager to learn more. I'm looking for the perfect partner. I've been badly treated in the past but I'm still a romantic at heart.'

On Talk Radio with Derek Hatton I was discussing Carlisle's latest escape when I mentioned that Michael Knighton and the Carlisle fans didn't have the closest relationship. An hour later my mobile rang. It was Knighton. It was the first time I'd heard from him since our transfer discussions a year earlier. So he hadn't lost my number after all.

'I'm ringing to tick you off,' he said.

'Pardon?'

'A journalist has just been on to me. He's trying to make trouble with your comment that I don't get on with the players.'

I tried to explain that I hadn't said that, but there didn't seem much point in wasting my breath.

Carlisle appointed a new manager for 2000/01, Ian Atkins, the man who had tried to sign me for Chester a few weeks earlier. And Carlisle bought a player! Mark Birch was their first in three years. He cost £10,000. Carlisle arranged to pay the fee in instalments.

Swindon had finished bottom of Division One and Jimmy Quinn was sacked. A transfer ban was placed on the club because they couldn't pay their players' wages. In fact, the Inland Revenue came close to sending Swindon out of existence. The club's debt was in the region of £10 million. My £25,000 put me somewhere near the back of a very long queue. The PFA sent me two payments of £1,500 to tide me over while they waited for Swindon to come out of administration.

I thought about my trip to America with Bournemouth. With the bonus of my fame the year before, maybe a club over there might be interested? I wanted a new agent so I approached Rodney Marsh, the former QPR and England forward, who had played in the US and who was now involved in a new sports management company. We played tennis together and he said he'd try to get me something over there, so I signed with him. He went to the States and reported back: nothing doing. American clubs only get four work permits so they don't want foreign players unless they're David Beckham.

Clubs were coming back for pre-season training. I was working out in a London gym when I saw Stuart Murdoch, Wimbledon's goalkeeping coach. He invited me to train with the Dons. Their manager, Terry Burton, said it would be okay but he stressed there was nothing for me. Wimbledon's players made me feel welcome, but because I didn't have a contract I felt completely out of place. I felt inferior. I'd been training there for two weeks when one morning I let in the softest goal imaginable. I felt like an utter twat. I didn't go back. Being there was making me feel worse about myself.

At the end of July, Rodney Marsh spoke to Exeter City's manager, Noel Blake. Noel invited me for a two-day trial. It was strange to be asked to go on trial after playing more than 100 League games but I wasn't exactly snowed under with offers. After training there on Thursday and Friday, Noel asked me to play in a friendly on the Monday. On Monday morning I drove 200 miles back to Exeter from London. I was walking around the pitch when out came Arjan Van

Heusden, the second-choice keeper at Cambridge when I'd been there the previous season.

'Don't tell me you've just signed,' I said.

'Yeah, a two-year contract.'

I drove back to London, absolutely fuming, and rang Rodney. He told me to call Noel Blake and thank him for letting me train at Exeter. I'd had such bad press from Mel Machin and Jimmy Quinn, and Rodney thought I didn't need any more. I rang Noel and thanked him through gritted teeth. He said he'd tried to contact me, which was strange because my mobile was never switched off.

Billy Smith did manage to get through. Billy had been in charge at Carshalton when I'd played a couple of games for them on loan from Palace; now he was manager of Crawley Town in the Dr Martens Premier League, one level below the Conference. Crawley were playing Division Two Oxford United in a friendly and they needed a goalkeeper. I played, and after the match Billy had a word with Denis Smith, Oxford's manager. Denis had been in the Sky studio when I was Man of the Match for Bournemouth against Bristol City. Denis said he'd love to sign me but Richard Knight, the goalkeeper I had replaced at Carlisle, was established in Oxford's first team so they could only afford a reserve 'keeper's wage. I said, 'No problem, Denis. I won't be as expensive as you think.' Denis said he'd heard Jimmy Quinn slagging me off, but he couldn't find anyone to say a good word about Quinn so he gave me the benefit of the doubt. We agreed on £500 a week for a month then we'd see how things were going.

Oxford was yet another club with massive money problems. They had a colourful recent history, starting when Robert Maxwell took over in the early 1980s. Maxwell broke Football League rules by also buying a controlling interest in Oxford's local rivals Reading. He then tried to merge the clubs to form what he would have called Thames Valley Royals. When the League and the supporters of both clubs thwarted his plans, Maxwell bought Derby County and put his son in charge at Oxford. Maxwell senior also tried to buy Manchester United, Tottenham and Watford. Despite his track record, all these clubs were happy to talk to him – only failure to agree a deal, or Football League intervention, stopped Maxwell adding to his empire.

After Maxwell went for his final swim, Oxford went through a succession of owners. Contractors had built about one-third of a new stadium before it emerged that the club couldn't pay them. In December 1996 the builders moved off site for the longest Christmas break ever. Oxford were £13 million in debt. The best players were sold for less than their worth or given away under the Bosman ruling. Players received their wages courtesy of PFA loans. Non-playing staff worked without pay. Supporters delivered food parcels to the ground.

In February 1999 London hotelier Firoz Kassam bought Oxford for a pound and opened negotiations to get the stadium back on track. Kassam wouldn't release funds for the playing side until the ground was sorted out. He wanted to build a hotel and cinema along with the stadium but he didn't tell the fans that he was still going to invest in the team. They were starved of information, as usual. Chairmen never seem to think it's part of their job to tell the supporters what's happening.

The season before I arrived, Oxford had escaped relegation to Division Three by one point. They had a poor squad and were soon struggling again. They didn't even have a training ground. At five to ten we'd be given directions to a field or a school that we'd just heard was available. When the club did get their own training facilities the pitches were flooded and the goals were broken. It was no coincidence that Oxford were bottom of the league, as it usually isn't.

Richard Knight started the 2000/01 season in the firing line. Richard is one of those 'keepers who makes a mistake then gets up and starts screaming at his defenders. He was a lot more confident than I was at the time, even though I had five or six years' more experience. A few days after signing my month's contract I stumbled at home and turned my ankle. I missed the first couple of games, then Richard got injured. I played at Stoke, on painkillers and with my ankle strapped up. Stoke's first-team coach was Nigel Pearson. When Nigel saw me he grabbed me and gave me a big hug. 'I still can't believe it!' he said. His team wasn't quite as friendly. Stoke had eighteen efforts on target and won 4-0. The match, on 13 September 2000, was a few weeks after my twenty-seventh birthday. I never played another Football League game.

Richard Knight came back into the team. I gradually got fit, signed another month's contract and played in the reserves. In some ways that's more enjoyable than first-team football. If I want to dribble the ball around a forward in the reserves, I will; if I want to hit a long ball on the off-chance of my forward getting on the end if it, I will. When you do that in the first team you get hammered the first time it doesn't work. I could be Jimmy Glass in the reserves, coming for every cross and being loud and dominant. I found it hard to instil that confidence in the first team because I didn't feel it myself.

Then Oxford brought a Norwegian goalkeeper over, Clas Andre Guttulsrod. I asked him about the coaching in Norway. He said that every club has at least one goalkeeping coach and that former Liverpool 'keeper Ray Clemence does a summer school there. Yet Clas came over here to experience our wonderful coaching. Ray Clemence had told him that the training here is fantastic. That might be what Ray experienced when he played for England but he obviously wasn't familiar with my world. When foreign players arrive in our lower divisions they look brilliant, but give them a season or two of our facilities and they slump, so we bring some more over. I watched a Scottish First Division match on Sky and both teams had foreign goalkeepers. When I left Swindon I was willing to play for £500 a week but every door was blocked by a foreign 'keeper.

Once upon a time there was a Coventry City youth team. It included two men who went on to achieve national fame: David Icke and Michael Knighton. Later in life one of them attracted ridicule when his views were dismissed as the rantings of a madman. The other started to dress in turquoise and claimed to be a messenger of God.

David Icke was a goalkeeper in his Coventry days. A few years ago he wrote a newspaper article which asked 'Where have all the good goalkeepers gone?' He said England used to have great 'keepers, like Gordon Banks, Ray Clemence and Peter Shilton, but that standards have fallen, even though 'keepers get better coaching now. That made me laugh. David Icke's not alone. Everyone thinks the training today is brilliant, except those who have experienced it. Maybe Banks, Clemence and Shilton didn't get great coaching either. But football wasn't as money-based in those days so 'keepers got a game in the first team at sixteen and they didn't have television cameras covering every inch of their goal. 'Keepers were given a chance.

Oxford were rock-bottom of Division Two and I felt I deserved a call-up. At the beginning of October, Denis Smith resigned and Joe Kinnear was appointed director of football. Joe had little involvement with training. He looked for players to buy and left the coaching to

David Kemp, whom he'd brought in as first-team coach. I'd known David since my days at Palace and was confident about my future. Oxford were almost certain to be relegated but sometimes you have to go backwards to go forwards. The team needed rebuilding and I thought I had a good chance of being involved. David even had an outfield shirt made for me because he wanted the option of playing me as a striker.

Things were looking up. Work on Oxford's new stadium restarted after nearly four years. Joe Kinnear and Rodney Marsh negotiated a contract for me until the end of the season for £600 a week. It just needed to be written up and signed. And my settlement from Swindon finally arrived. When they had gone into administration it had looked as if I wouldn't get the £25,000 we had agreed. I threatened to sue them for the full amount of my contract, £140,000. We made another deal and they sent me a cheque for £40,000. When it arrived I was £50,000 in debt and the interest was spiralling every day. I gave Dad the £20,000 he had loaned me and paid off as much of my other debts as I could afford, but I still needed £10,000. Maybe I could win it?

Richard Knight was losing confidence because Oxford were getting hammered every week. In December David Kemp played me at Brentford in the LDV Vans Trophy. We lost 4-1. I made a mistake with the last goal, a quick free-kick which I couldn't hold. I wasn't happy about conceding four goals but it was going to take more than one game to find my feet. This was only my fourth first-team match in a year. I went to see David the next day. He didn't think I'd played well; I didn't look like a 'keeper who had played 100 League games. I like David, but I thought that was ignorant of him. You need two or three matches to get your eye in, especially in goal and in a team that's playing badly. I didn't hear any more about my contract. That was my chance: one game.

With hindsight, I can see that Swindon killed my career. The good work I'd done at Bournemouth went out of the window. After leaving Swindon, with Jimmy Quinn's comments plastered over the papers, I had to prove myself all over again. You can't do that in ninety minutes. Within days of the LDV Vans game, Oxford signed Neil Cutler on loan from Aston Villa. He went straight into the first team. Richard Knight was on the bench and playing in the reserves. I was training with the youth team. Neil Cutler was Oxford's fifth goalkeeper in less than half a season. The team had won two League games out of twenty. Could it be the poor training facilities? What about the coaching? No, it must be the 'keeper.

At the end of 2000 Michael Knighton resigned as Carlisle chairman. The decision was forced on him by the Department of Trade and Industry, which banned Knighton from being a company director for five and a half years. His wife was banned for two years. The DTI acted after a private school in Huddersfield owned by the Knightons went bust, owing nearly £500,000. The couple admitted paying their holding company in preference to other creditors, in particular the Inland Revenue.

The ban made it illegal for the Knightons to have any input in the running of Carlisle United. The club was left with only two directors, one being the former secretary, the other being Mark Knighton, the owner's twenty-three-year-old son. Knighton senior still owned ninety-three per cent of the shares, although of course he wouldn't dream of exerting any influence over the club. Several months into the ban a mobile-phone bill was leaked to the *Carlisle News & Star*. It showed that Mark Knighton regularly rang his father during office hours, often several times a day.

Carlisle were drawn at home to Arsenal in the FA Cup third round. Oxford didn't have a game that day. I told a *News & Star* journalist that I wouldn't mind going up to Brunton Park with Louise. The last Carlisle match I'd been to was the one I scored in, nearly two years earlier. The journalist said he would get it organised. He rang me a few days before the game and told me that everyone he'd spoken to at the club had said the same thing: 'Sorry, all the tickets have been sold.' He was about to write an article revealing that Carlisle United couldn't find a seat for the man who had kept them in the Football League. The club suddenly produced two tickets. I like to think they weren't being malicious; the last couple of years had taught me it was more likely to be incompetence. And on that score things were about to get much worse.

On my previous visit to Carlisle they had been celebrating the Great Escape. The club had survived the next season on goal difference and were now bottom of Division Three yet again, six points adrift.

Financial problems meant that Ian Atkins had not been able to sign any players until a few days before the season started. He'd had to take what was left, which wasn't much. The Arsenal match was a welcome distraction. The result could hardly have mattered less. Carlisle fans would have happily swapped victory against the team who were second in the Premiership for three League points. All 15,000 tickets had sold out in a day, showing the potential that for years had been wasted.

Now, at last, this potential was about to be realised. A takeover deal had been announced that week. Carlisle United was under new ownership. Michael Knighton had sold his shares to a company called Mamcarr and a millionaire businessman called Stephen Brown. I was introduced to Mr Brown in the directors' bar before the game. With his moustache and ample waistline he was a dead ringer for Knighton. Brown asked me if I wanted a drink. He went behind the bar and poured me half a lager. 'I'd like to have a chat with you before you go,' he said. It sounded promising. I would consider going back to Carlisle now that Knighton was leaving.

I agreed to do the half-time draw. That wasn't for the club, it was for me. After the year I'd had it was wonderful to soak up an ovation from 15,000 people. They had to virtually drag me off the pitch. The bloke who won the draw unzipped his jacket. His T-shirt said: 'May 8, 1999: I Was There.' Me too.

Carlisle lost the match 1-0. Not bad against a team ninety places above them. After the game Stephen Brown pulled me aside.

'Give me a call next week,' he said.

'OK, Stephen. I'll do that. Cheers.'

Louise couldn't believe the reaction I got from Carlisle fans. She'd only seen the fag end of my career so it was nice to show her that I had achieved something. Grown men were in tears and hugging me in the street. One bloke stopped dead, gasped, and threw his arms around me. 'It's Jimmy Glass! I can't believe it! Jimmy! Thank you!' I could have solved all my money troubles there and then by holding a car-boot sale and flogging my personal belongings. Should I go to Carlisle on a more permanent basis? It was a long way from home. It was usually freezing. But I could live with the adulation.

The following week Stephen Brown's face loomed large in every national newspaper and on every news bulletin. The 'millionaire businessman' was an unemployed curry-house waiter. He had spent the past few years turning up at football and rugby clubs around Scotland claiming to have inherited millions of pounds and offering to invest it. He enjoyed the clubs' hospitality for a few weeks while they waited in vain for a glimpse of his wallet. Brown had driven to the press conference to announce his 'investment' in Carlisle United straight after signing on at his local dole office. 'I thought it was a bit strange that a millionaire would be driving a clapped-out Cavalier,' said one of his previous victims.

In hindsight it's easy to say that something about Stephen Brown didn't seem quite right – the way he strolled behind the bar and expertly pulled pints, for example. But I was completely taken in by him. He was one hell of a conman and he must have enjoyed lording it at the Arsenal match. The thought of someone conning Michael Knighton is priceless.

Mamcarr, the company which had supposedly bought the rest of Knighton's shares, was next to come under media scrutiny. Knighton would not reveal Mamcarr's identity. The newspapers pointed out that 'Mamcarr' bears a strong resemblance to the initials of Knighton and his closest family: Michael, Anne, Mark, Chevonne, Anna, Rosemary, Rory. Carlisle MP Eric Martlew raised the takeover in the House of Commons and he called in the DTI, the Football Association and the Football League. The FA raided Brunton Park and removed documents. The *News & Star* revealed that Knighton Holdings had used Brunton Park as security to raise a £1 million loan the day after Michael Knighton had supposedly sold his shares in Carlisle United. Carlisle were losing £25,000 a week. This was a business which had raised millions of pounds in player sales during the past few years and spent next to nothing on transfer fees. Where had all the money gone?

Michael Knighton was interviewed for a Radio Five investigation into the ownership of football clubs. The reporter suggested that the Mamcarr deal was designed to let Knighton keep control of Carlisle behind the smokescreen of a company which existed in name only. Knighton switched off the reporter's tape recorder. On the same programme a Football League spokesman said it wasn't proven that Knighton had broken any ownership rules. As the programme went on it emerged that there are virtually no rules; anyone can come along, buy a League club and do whatever they like with it, regardless of the cost to the club and the community. The FA spokesman only came to life when the presenter introduced him as 'Dave'. 'That's David, if you don't mind.'

Every week we read about FA inquiries because a player raised his hand to an opponent or kicked the ball away after the whistle had gone. When Robbie Savage played for Leicester City he was hauled in front of an FA committee for using the toilet in the referee's room. But what are the FA doing about all those clubs – their members – being shafted by the people who should be looking after them? Brighton: their former owners secretly sold the ground for huge profit and left the club homeless. Doncaster Rovers: their former owner had already bought Bridlington Town, sold the ground and closed the club down. Then, with no hint of concern from football's authorities, he bought Doncaster and hired someone to burn down the stand as an insurance scam. The lower divisions must be taken away from chairmen who are only in it for the buck.

I was driving four hours a day to train with Oxford's youth team. At the end of January 2001 I rang David Kemp and told him I wouldn't be coming in any more. I had to try to get first-team football. I started phoning clubs myself to ask if they needed a goalkeeper. My agents didn't like that; they thought it made them look bad. It might have done, but I had to do something. Some managers talked to me, others wouldn't even take my call. I rang George Graham at Tottenham. Their goalkeeper, Ian Walker, was in the papers saying he wanted to leave because he wasn't being treated well, which is quite amusing from someone who was picking up thousands of pounds every week. George sounded surprised that I had the audacity to ask him, but I thought, if you wanted to say hello to me at that golf day two years ago you can tell me you're all right for a goalkeeper now. I must have been having a confident day. Some days I was scared to pick up the phone. I didn't want to be knocked back any more.

I rang Crystal Palace to ask if I could train with them. Alan Smith was back there as manager. He said no, it wouldn't be fair on a trialist they were looking at. For a couple of weeks I trained at Brentford. I was reluctant, bearing in mind the way Ron Noades had treated me, but I like the Brentford boys. Then I found a club. Billy Smith of Crawley Town rang me to say his 'keeper was injured and did I fancy a game? I'd come full circle. Ten years after playing for Billy's Carshalton team as a seventeen-year-old, I was back in non-League football. It was an easy decision, though. It was great just to play. I played four games for Crawley until their 'keeper got fit.

During one match a fan said, 'What are you doing here, Jimmy?'

'I'm just having a game. I'm just trying to enjoy it. What's the point of being a footballer if you don't play football?'

In November 2001 the Bishop of Oxford performed an exorcism on the pitch at Oxford United's new stadium. Gypsies had been evicted from the site when the football club had bought it. The club was struggling in Division Three. Could it be the poor training facilities? What about the coaching? No, it must be the gypsies' curse.

Thirteen

NON-LEAGUE

I saved Carlisle from the Conference, but I couldn't save myself. At the end of February 2001 I had a call from Geoff Chapple, the manager of Conference club Kingstonian. The 'keeper they had on loan from Spurs was going back; Geoff asked if I was interested in replacing him. My parents' house is just a couple of miles from Kingstonian's ground. I needed money, and trying to help my local club seemed like a good way to earn it. I signed until the end of the season for £400 a week.

As non-League clubs go it could have been a lot worse. Geoff Chapple was arguably the most successful manager in non-League football. He'd joined Kingstonian in 1997 and taken the club into the Conference for the first time. They'd also won the FA Trophy at Wembley two years running. This season, 2000/01, was Kingstonian's third in the Conference. They had just received national exposure for their best-ever FA Cup run. They beat Brentford and Southend and came within seconds of knocking out Bristol City for a place in the fifth round. But reproducing that form in the Conference was proving difficult. They were in the relegation zone, third from bottom. Here we go again. When a goalkeeper is struggling for confidence it would be good for him to play a few games for a good team and enjoy some quiet afternoons; instead he finds himself at a struggling club, spending ninety minutes at the wrong end of a shooting gallery.

Kingstonian – or K's as their fans call them – had a couple of familiar faces. I used to clean Mark Harris's boots as a YTS trainee at Palace, and Eddie Akuamoah had been my strike partner as a kid for Raynes Park Rovers. My first match was at home to Hednesford on 3 March. It's just as well we weren't away to Hednesford because I had no idea where it was. K's were three points from safety. Hednesford were one point behind us. We were winning 1-0 when they forced a last-minute corner. I was organising my defence when I noticed a figure in a green top running up the pitch. It was Hednesford's goalkeeper. I just laughed. Even now I don't expect the 'keeper to score. And he didn't. As we walked off at the end, we shook hands. 'Well, you did it, you git,' he said, 'so I thought I'd try my luck.'

That was Kingstonian's first home league win for five months. The next Saturday we had Morecambe at home, and lost 6-1. The good news is that I couldn't be blamed for all six goals; the bad news is that I was sent off at 4-1. A Morecambe forward had come charging towards me while my defenders thought about strolling back. I went down at the striker's feet. He fell over me and I was shown the red card for the first time in my career. That game hit me hard. Afterwards Mum suggested I find a better team. I spelled out the situation as I saw it: 'Nobody else wants me – I'm shit!'

Three days later K's bounced back with a 1-0 win at Telford. I played really well that night but I was barracked by the home fans throughout the game. At the final whistle I turned to them and cheered. When I got to the tunnel some bloke spat at me. I gave him a squirt from my water bottle. I got lots of abuse at Kingstonian. 'Getting people relegated again are you, Glass? Whatever you do don't come and play for us next season!' People thought I'd taken Swindon and Oxford down when I'd only played a few matches. Wherever I went fans picked up on the goal. Some gave me a cheer, others gave me stick. Maybe they got a kick out of seeing me brought back down to size.

It soon became clear that Kingstonian had professional ambitions while being run on an amateur basis. The only training facility was a five-a-side pitch they rented from a local college. I was also training at Brentford, but most of the K's players had full-time jobs. What can you do for an hour and a half one or two nights a week? There was no time to focus on tactics and work as a team, and it showed most Saturdays.

If crosses aren't stopped and opponents aren't marked, you've got problems. 'We can't keep making mistakes!' was often heard during post-match inquests. But the lack of preparation meant we couldn't help making mistakes. I felt sorry for these players who weren't being coached but were being slated if they didn't perform. Players were hiding. They were often relieved to be left out of the team. The only person really hurt by Kingstonian's plight was Geoff Chapple. Geoff is an excellent motivator, which is why his teams do so well against

League clubs in the FA Cup. But he was struggling to cope with the changing face of football.

The shadow of professional football was hanging over Kingstonian. Some players had dropped out of the professional game but were still on big money, which is ridiculous for a club with average crowds of 1,000. Raising themselves to go to Northwich on a Tuesday night was beyond them. Maybe that's why they were forced into non-League. After defeats I saw twenty-year-olds gloating in the bar with a pint of lager in their hand. 'I'm all right. I've got a three-year contract and I'm picking up £600 a week.'

That's what happens when money is allowed to take over. When Sky's millions began flowing into football the first batch of players laughed their heads off. 'Can you believe this? They're giving me twenty grand a week!' The next batch thought they actually deserved it. Players everywhere wanted it. Money became the motivating factor.

The only players worth massive money are those who put bums on seats, the likes of David Beckham and Michael Owen. Paying somebody for what they do on the pitch is great. By all means give players incentives for scoring goals or keeping clean sheets. But instead, clubs pay people for what they might do, if the wind's blowing in the right direction. Youngsters who have scored ten goals only have to sign one contract to be made for life. Some of them have just left school. Young men who look half-decent should not be on £3,000 a week. Kids will start for £300 if it gives them the chance of a career.

For more than a decade clubs have been throwing the Sky windfall straight down the drain instead of using it to develop young talent. Players go to a club and fail, then go to another club and fail again, picking up money from chairmen who are desperate to throw it at them. You can't blame players for taking it, but this policy has ruined dozens of clubs, clubs whose youth systems aren't good enough to produce their own players and whose coaching isn't good enough to improve older players. They have few options other than panic buying.

As more money flows into football, more clubs find themselves in debt. Division One clubs spend all they have, and a lot more, on the gamble of reaching the Premiership. The financial strategy of most Football League clubs seems to have been based on a philosophy similar to mine in the casino: 'We know there's money out there so let's risk everything we've got in the hope of getting it.' Chairmen throw money at the manager and say, 'Get us promoted', but it means nothing without the foundations of good facilities and coaching.

Premiership clubs can afford these. Lower down the divisions it's the same old story. Clubs are in financial trouble because they've paid inflated wages. Then they skimp on youth development because they don't have enough money. They don't have enough money because they don't develop young players to sell. They don't develop young players so they have to buy.

The FA should take back the three divisions of the Football League, turn the Conference into a Fourth Division and leave the Premiership to it. The Premiership has too much power to change, but lessons can be learned and applied in the Football League. Clubs need the stability of a sensibly run league where they can't get millions of pounds in debt and have to beg the fans to bail them out. Every club should have to have local players comprise half their squad. Clubs would then find and develop players from their community rather than give another handout to the mercenaries. There has to be a change in mentality. Football has to be about sport again rather than business. If you take the sport out of football, what are you left with?

The only thing in football you can't put a price on is fans' loyalty, but that loyalty is being stretched to breaking point by clubs and players in relentless pursuit of money. Kingstonian was a prime example. K's had banked big cheques from televised FA Cup matches and two Wembley visits but they were still in a mess thanks to the 'I'm all right, I'm on £600 a week' brigade.

Manchester United *v*. Bayern Munich – the rematch. In April 2001, two years after United's Champions League final triumph, the teams met again in the semi-final first leg. That night also saw another echo from the summer of 1999: Jimmy Glass *v*. Scarborough. It was the first time I'd played against the team I kicked out of the Football League. If this had been the day after my goal I would have been lynched; two years on, I didn't know what to expect. Things hadn't gone too well for either of us. Scarborough were in their second Conference season and they had adapted to non-League mediocrity without much trouble.

Their fans barracked me a bit – 'Jimmy Glass takes it up the arse!' – but on the whole they were fine. I was waiting for their supporters to do something or for a player to rip into me, but it never happened. In the bar afterwards a couple of Scarborough fans came up to me. 'We shouldn't really be talking to you,' they said, 'but never mind.' It was the first time I'd spoken to any Scarborough supporters. It was good to get my feelings off my chest. I hope they realised I was a normal person doing a job. Every action has an equal and opposite reaction. While my goal sparked joy in Cumbria it ruined the dreams of a lot of people on the other side of the country.

Four days later Kingstonian played Yeovil. They were managed by Colin Addison, the manager at Scarborough when I sent them down. When he saw me before the match he said, 'Oh, it's you, is it?' He made light of it. I wanted to sit down and speak to him but he didn't seem that bothered. To him it was gone. Maybe it isn't the kind of thing you want to talk about when you're on the wrong end of it.

Not everyone connected with Scarborough could let go so easily. I saw an interview in the *Non-League Paper* with John Russell, Scarborough's chairman when they were relegated. He said it's strange how something you love so much can suddenly turn sour. When Scarborough went down Russell lost the club to creditors. He became depressed and didn't get out of bed for four months. 'What happened that day is still a nightmare,' he said. 'You can budget for a lot of things, but not that. It was my life and, basically, something that happened in that 97th minute virtually cost me my life. I still have nightmares over it and I think I always will... I feel that I would have gone to the gutter completely, I would have lost it. I would have ended up in a permanent home, or probably I would have ended up taking my life.' I had to put the paper down. I felt so frustrated that I'd sent someone into depression while helping Michael Knighton. I tried to apply some perspective, telling myself that football isn't that important. But it's hard for anyone who loves their club to see it that way.

How important is football? That's something I asked myself a lot when my life was on hold for the sake of trying to get a game. To Carlisle fans deep in stoppage time, football is everything. And yet it really is only a game. There are worse things than your football team losing. There are worse things than your football team going out of the League. It's not that football is unimportant to those who love it, but there's more to life. For a long time, my problem was that there wasn't more to my life.

★

Towards the end of the season I started keeping clean sheets. I kept five in my fourteen matches for Kingstonian and saved three penalties. But the team wasn't scoring. There were too many negative tactics, too much emphasis on not conceding a goal. If we let one in it was seen as a disaster. People's expectations of me were massive. I was expected to make no mistakes at Conference level because I was supposed to have had ten years of professional coaching. I felt I had to be twice as good as the other team's 'keeper, especially since my goal. If I made an error, that became the newspaper headline. Since the goal I'm always going to be a story, whether a positive or a negative one. Making the *Sun* and the *Mail* retract their articles about me probably made it more likely to be negative. I was nervous before every game at Kingstonian because I felt every mistake would be blown out of proportion. When the opposition were attacking I'd sometimes think, 'Please don't shoot – I might miss it' or 'Please don't cross – I might drop it.'

People sensed that I lacked confidence. I heard whispers that some of the directors thought I wasn't doing a good enough job. I wasn't brilliant, but I was the best they were going to get in their position. Dad couldn't watch me at Kingstonian. He'd heard the murmurs that I didn't play well enough. I said to him, 'What's wrong with you? It's just a game. Come and enjoy it.' He came to the last couple of matches and pretended to enjoy it, but he didn't. The ups and downs were the killer for him. One minute it's great, the next his son is ridiculed in the papers for his friends to see. Even when the ups and downs are relatively minor – if you're in the team then out of the team – it can be difficult; that all becomes magnified many times if you're world news one minute and unemployed the next. Footballers' families get it worse than the players. They're on the rollercoaster as well but they can't do anything about it. Two years after running around the house in ecstasy when my goal flashed up on television, Dad couldn't watch a match. Is that one moment worth two years of misery? Some people might say it is. He might say it is. But those two years made him bitter about football. I was trying hard not to feel the same way.

Kingstonian were relegated at the end of April, on a Thursday night in Chester. We needed a win to have any chance of staying up. In stoppage time it was 0-0 and the Kingstonian fans behind my goal were urging me upfield. While I'm a great believer in football, I'm also a realist. I don't for one second think that every time a club is in trouble

I'll run up and slap in the winning goal. I saved a penalty that night and played out of my skin as a goalkeeper. I didn't see why I should try to score the winner if the rest of the team couldn't. At Carlisle I felt I owed Nigel Pearson for having faith in me. I didn't have that feeling about Kingstonian – and I didn't want to run up the pitch and fail.

The rest of the team stayed in the north for a game on Saturday. I went back on the supporters' coach because I had an appointment in London the next day. It was a long way home. After saving Carlisle, and having left just before the last rites at Swindon and Oxford, relegation had finally caught up with me. Some of the supporters were philo-sophical about Kingstonian's fate. A couple of the younger ones were really angry. I said to one of them, 'Listen, mate, it's only a game. There's people dying in this world.'

'Er, yeah, I suppose so...'

They stopped talking. I don't know if they agreed with me or if they just wanted me to shut up. At least they cared. Most of the players had been resigned to relegation when I got there, even with sixteen games left. I went to Kingstonian with a genuine desire to help my local club. I left with no feeling for them. I had thought it was just professional football that treats players badly. Later in the year Kingstonian went into administration with debts of £1 million. Nine players were sacked. Simon Stewart, the captain, only found out when his P45 arrived through the post.

Fourteen

FAREWELL, FOOTBALL

As Kingstonian were being relegated, Carlisle were in their third consecutive fight to stay in the League. I had a call from Alan Steel of CCUIST, the newly formed Carlisle supporters' trust. Dozens of trusts have sprung up at Football League clubs in recent years. They aim to buy fans a seat on the board, giving clubs a financial boost and support-ers a voice. Anything which gives fans some influence has to be welcomed, but they shouldn't have to buy representation. It's their club. Supporters pay their money every week and should be entitled to a say.

Carlisle's trust pledged to invest in the club only on the condition that the Knighton family was no longer involved. For the past few years Michael Knighton had said he was desperate to sell Carlisle. He claimed he was hanging on only because no one wanted to buy, yet Alan Steel knew of several attempts to buy the club in the previous eighteen months. One interested party spent £50,000 on legal fees preparing his bid. All potential buyers said negotiations were going well, until Michael Knighton put further conditions on the table at the last minute which scuppered the deal.

The Arsenal FA Cup tie in January 2001 had sparked a revival in Carlisle's League form. They clinched survival in the second-to-last match of the season. By the club's recent standards that counted as a stress-free campaign. Since Christmas, Ian Atkins' team had shown play-off form, mainly thanks to some inspired loan signings. For the first time in years Carlisle looked capable of rising above the scrap for survival. This all changed during the summer. Carlisle's board, half of which was Michael Knighton's son Mark, refused to sign any of the loan players who had made such a difference. Without these men the squad consisted mainly of untried youngsters. Scott Dobie, the only rising star, was sold to West Brom for a cut-price £150,000. After three seasons of Carlisle fighting for Football League survival, and still no prospect of an end to the Knighton regime, CCUIST asked its members if they would support a boycott of home matches during the coming season. Three-quarters said they would.

When Carlisle's few remaining players reported back for pre-season training, four of them were called into director Andrea Whitaker's office. She told them they were sacked. The reason? The club had decided they were earning too much. Ian Atkins was left with just five players who had played in the Football League. It was the final straw, and he resigned. A few days later the players were reinstated when the PFA warned that the sackings were illegal. The fans felt that the sackings were a ploy to drive Ian Atkins out because he had dared to criticise his lack of boardroom support, but a club statement blamed the sackings on the proposed fans' boycott. Then it emerged that the sackings had been planned at the end of the previous season, two months before anyone had even mentioned a boycott. Michael Knighton began a philosophy degree at Durham University. The syllabus included 'ethics and values'.

I signed with a new agent, Andy Evans. Richard Knight at Oxford had recommended him. I'd realised that Rodney Marsh's company deals more with sports celebrities than with the nitty-gritty of getting players fixed up with clubs. Gary Johnson, Yeovil Town's new manager, rang and asked to have a look at me. Yeovil were the biggest non-League club in Britain and had just been pipped to the Conference's promotion spot by Rushden. This wasn't good enough for Yeovil's board, who sacked manager Colin Addison. Yeovil is only thirty miles from Bournemouth, where Louise lived, so I thought it would be ideal. In my two days there I made a point of making my presence felt, leaping around all over the place and bellowing orders. At the end of the second day Gary told me he'd signed Jon Sheffield from Plymouth. My goalkeeping style was 'too angry'.

As my career ground to a halt my self-destructive streak grew stronger than ever. If I wasn't near a casino I'd go into betting shops and put money on dogs. I knew nothing about them but that didn't stop me betting on combinations – number one to win that race, number six the next – because the odds were better. Betting shops were a poor substitute for casinos, though. I spent hours in the Stakis in

Bournemouth and the Grosvenor in Knightsbridge, London, waiting for the next card, the one that would make me big money. I ploughed on through terrible losing streaks because I knew my luck would turn. Sometimes it never did. I'd run to the bank and get a couple of grand out. An hour or so later I'd be back for more.

The Grosvenor opened at two in the afternoon. Sometimes I'd be waiting outside, counting down the minutes; sometimes I was the last to leave when they closed the doors at four o'clock the next morning. A fourteen-hour shift in the casino can be a hard day at the office. It was always the same faces. One day they'd be happy and chirpy, the next like death warmed up. I got talking to one bloke who just watched the fruit machines. They had a £1,000 jackpot and he was always trying to spot one that hadn't paid out all day. I'd give him £50 to play. One day he pulled the jackpot and gave me £500. If I was doing well I'd give the waitresses £100 for a glass of Coke, just to see their expressions.

I met some really nice people. The casino staff probably thought I was a decent bloke, but a mug. What else could they think after watching me blow a month's wages on a hand of cards time after time? I tried to look as if it wasn't hurting but they could see straight through me. If I was winning some of them would whisper, 'Take your money – just go!' They had nothing to gain by seeing me lose. It wasn't their money. When I had a bad loss I could see they were gutted. But that summer I hit a winning streak. Four kings won me £2,000. A spin of the roulette wheel won me £3,000. In one week I won £21,000, including £11,000 in a night. At one point there was £14,000 in a shoebox on top of my wardrobe. I put it all in the bank and told Louise I'd cleared my debts, which had been £20,000.

Some gamblers know what they're doing. They can work out the odds or they can tell which cards are coming. I wasn't that clever. The only skill I could have nurtured was knowing when to quit. But I wasn't that clever either. My hot streak continued as I won £7,000 in two hours – and then kept going until I'd blown the lot. The tide had turned. Within a few days I'd lost another £21,000. I was back to square one. I didn't tell Louise because I was scared she would leave me.

During pre-season in July 2001 I returned to Brentford to train. I tried hard, but the feeling of inferiority that had plagued me at Wimbledon a year earlier surfaced again. The worst thing was that I'd grown up with a lot of the Brentford boys. I was among friends but I still felt as if I didn't belong. One Friday morning the team was preparing for a friendly the next day. I had to sit on the sidelines and watch the first-team 'keeper doing the things I used to do. That hurt me.

There were no phone calls, not even from non-League clubs. My options were disappearing. I could see three possible reasons for managers' lack of interest: I'm a crap goalkeeper, managers don't like me as a person, or my reputation precedes me courtesy of Jimmy Quinn and Mel Machin. Managers I'd never met said they didn't fancy me, even when I'd played well against their teams. John Granville, my 'keeper coach at Swindon, was trying to find a club for me and he spoke to Barry Fry at Peterborough. Barry told him that Jimmy Quinn had slated me. Mel Machin had been telling people I was a bad trainer. Maybe I should have told Machin about the training I'd had to arrange for myself at Fulham because the coaching at Bournemouth was so poor. I had the idea of approaching Bournemouth as a goalkeeping coach. I was also still young enough to play if required, and they would get the whole package for £500 a week. I went down there but got the vibe that it wouldn't work. Machin was director of football and I would have been setting myself up for another kick in the teeth.

'Don't give up,' Steve Coppell advised. 'You're still a young man.' Steve has always encouraged me, ever since he handed me my tracksuit when I was a fourteen-year-old at Palace. I regret not saying to him, 'Thanks for believing in me.' When most people get close to me they lose faith a bit. It's very difficult to believe that I'm just unlucky. They think, 'It can't be everyone else's fault. It must be you.' Maybe they're right. There were times when I should have kept my mouth shut and times when I should have worked harder, but that's difficult when you're living out of your car for clubs which show you no respect.

There was no money coming in but I never signed on the dole. I always thought someone would realise I was a good goalkeeper. Even so, my parents were starting to talk about 'a proper job'. Perhaps they had a point. In the two years since my goal I had played just eleven League games.

I thought about charging for personal appearances in Carlisle. But I'd always done everything for free and asking for money would have felt tacky. After a lot of soul-searching I decided to move to Bournemouth and look for a job. I didn't want to stop playing football, but to have a chance of doing it I'd have to keep waiting by the phone and be ready to drive to some distant town at a moment's notice. There's more to life than travelling the country chasing a game of football. I'd been doing that for eighteen months, for any club that showed a whiff of interest. It wasn't worth the stress on myself and my family. Louise couldn't make plans because she didn't know where I would be from one day to the next. I was finally realising that the people who care about me are more important than football. At the age of twenty-seven, I walked away from the game.

I visited a few recruitment agencies in Bournemouth. I told one woman, 'I'm an ex-footballer and I need a job.' She looked at me blankly and said, 'We've got vacancies in box-packing.' I spoke to a friend who worked in recruitment. He said, 'How do you fancy IT sales?' I said, 'What's that?'

IT sales turned out to be selling computer systems. This seemed to be the best way for someone with no experience of the 'real world' to earn money. In August, the need for money became even more urgent: Louise told me she was pregnant. I was thrilled – and frightened. I owed £25,000 and Lou thought I'd cleared my debts. I didn't tell her the truth. We wanted to keep the baby and I didn't want money worries to affect our decision. My friend in recruitment arranged an interview for me as a PC sales executive with Spire, an IT company near Bournemouth. I got the job.

It was hard to walk away from something I knew into something I knew nothing about. Did I have any abilities apart from catching a football? My first day at Spire was like my first day at school: 'This is James. He's starting today.' People couldn't understand what I was doing there. On my first day I built a computer from scratch. When I went to punch holes in the instruction manual, I couldn't work out how to use the hole-punch.

Season 2001/02 kicked off without me. Then my former Bournemouth teammate John Bailey called. John had scored Bournemouth's goal at Wembley three years earlier. Now he was playing for Brockenhurst in the Jewson Wessex League, three levels below the Conference. Brockenhurst is a small town in the New Forest, ten miles from Bournemouth. Their goalkeeper was injured so I agreed to play a few matches for £100 a week. Although I'd given up on professional foot-ball, or it had given up on me, I was glad just to get a game.

There are obvious differences between Brockenhurst's level and the Football League. The players aren't as fit or as tactically aware, and after each game the secretary hands you an envelope with your money. But the similarities with League clubs are frightening. Even at that level, clubs were blowing big money on wages instead of thinking about their infrastructure.

Brockenhurst's 'keeper soon got himself fit again, and the next call came from Salisbury City of the Dr Martens Premier League. Their goalkeeper was injured – could I play a few matches? In case of emer-gency, take Glass. My debut came on the evening of 11 September 2001. That afternoon I'd watched the hijacked planes fly into the World Trade Centre; that night all I could think about was my disappoint-ment that Salisbury had been beaten 3-0 by Tiverton.

The following Saturday we played at Kettering, and lost 4-0. Comments from the home fans behind my goal included, 'You're that shit goalkeeper!' I'd had enough. I didn't need this any more, not for £100 a week. That was the last serious game of football I ever played. I drove back with one of Salisbury's coaching staff and said to him, 'You don't belong to a Sunday team, do you?' He played for one near Wareham, just down the road from Bournemouth. 'Do you need a striker for tomorrow morning?'

The next day I played up front for Sandford in the Dorset Sunday League, and scored two goals. Then I linked up with Broadway Sports in division three of the Bournemouth Sunday League, paying my £3 subs every week. We won two of our matches 8-1 and 10-1. Some of these teams get battered every match but their players still love football so much. That's what I was like as a kid, conceding ten goals for Raynes Park Rovers and coming back for more. Love of the game was some-thing I had to try and rediscover.

I always played as a striker, working the frustrated forward out of my system after so many years. I scored six goals in two consecutive matches. One of them came after three seconds, straight from the kick-off, and is a contender for the fastest goal ever. In some ways my new role was a goalkeeper's revenge. I wanted to show that it's easier to score goals than to save them, so the first thing I did when I quit playing was to go out and prove that.

Being a goalkeeper hadn't been enjoyable for a long time. I wanted people to look at me with admiration and respect again, and playing in goal couldn't give me that any more. I'd been reduced to playing behind such bad defences that my confidence and motivation had gone. But I could still get respect by banging in goals and hearing the crowd say, 'Look at that!', even if the crowd was just some bloke walking his dog through a public park.

I still enjoy making a save more than scoring a goal, though. Maybe I'm a masochist because I like the pressure of playing in goal. When things go right there's nothing better. But if I had my time again I'd be a striker. Strikers can miss ten chances and it's all forgotten when they score one. With goalkeepers, the reverse is true. You can save everything except one shot and it might not be enough. Make one mistake and you're the villain. The only time I had any glory as a 'keeper was those few seconds at Carlisle when I tore up the rule book and played as a striker. Goalkeepers can't win.

If I'd stayed at Swindon, that first year I spent selling PCs I would have earned £60,000 plus bonuses. Instead, I was on £18,000, working nine hours a day for £70. When I should have been in the prime of my football career I was selling computer systems. I'm not embarrassed about that but I sometimes wonder how it happened. Every decision seemed right at the time. And yet I sit in my office, so frustrated with how things turned out.

One of my customers at Spire was Mel Machin. He rang me wanting a laptop computer. At first I thought someone was winding me up, but that deadpan delivery could only have been his. Machin sometimes seems to have a split personality. When you get him away from football and talking about his family or golf, he's a different person. I looked at him and thought, 'You used to stitch me up and tell people I was shit.' But I couldn't hate him. Football screws lots of us up in one way or another.

It was nice to be around people after months spent sitting at home, although working from nine till six every day was a daunting prospect after years of ten till twelve-thirty. You don't appreciate what you've got until you lose it. For ten years as a professional footballer I spent my afternoons playing snooker or tennis, sleeping or shopping. I could have been a nine-to-five footballer. I could have trained or studied every afternoon, but I never developed myself, as a footballer or as a person. The older players' lifestyle was all I knew.

I was determined to use what I'd learned from football in business. The main lesson is that you can't rely on people to help you. I wasted years waiting to be coached when I should have taken it on myself to do my own training and not expected other people to bring out the best in me. Now if I don't know something I'll make sure I find out. If I'm doing something wrong I want to be told so I can do it right. I want to progress to the best of my ability. The job is tedious – I sit behind a desk all day and talk to people about computer upgrades – but there's no running away if things go wrong, not with a family to support.

With Louise expecting a baby we needed money quickly for a house. If I officially retired from professional football on medical grounds, because of my wrists, I could cash in my PFA pension. That's what I did. My pension contributions were worth £20,000. The PFA sent me the money, and I blew £5,000 of it on cards. Self-inflicted wounds were still bleeding me dry. That autumn Louise discovered she was expecting twins. More excitement, more fear. We bought a house in Dorset, but only just. Louise was relying on me to sort things out. I still hadn't told her about my debts because I didn't want to risk her health, and because I was scared. I didn't tell her that I'd taken out an overdraft to pay the deposit. It came through the day before we were due to move in.

Jack and Ella were born on 25 March 2002. Nothing could have prepared me for their arrival. I wanted them to be perfect, and they were. I held them and started welling up. I was in awe of them at first. I didn't know what do with them. I just knew they were all right, they were safe. I felt I could take on the world.

A few afternoons later I went to the casino with £500. I'd sworn I wouldn't gamble once the twins were born. But this wasn't for excitement. It was desperation. I couldn't see another way out. After an hour I walked away with £5,000, but whatever I had was never enough. I went back that night and lost the lot. My self-control and self-respect had gone a long time ago. That should have been the best week of my life; instead, it was the worst. If I'm just beating myself up I can live with that, but not if I'm hurting the people who need me.

I kept gambling for the next few months. Then Louise rang me at work one day to ask why we weren't getting any bank statements. I couldn't hide the truth any more. I was either going to stop gambling or lose my children. Louise thought we had a few grand in the bank; I told her we owed £22,000. Since leaving Swindon I had blown more than £100,000.

That night we drove to my parents and told them everything. Mum and Dad never cease to amaze me. Dad got another loan and I negotiated repayments with the bank. My parents understood the stress I had been through and that was all I could have asked for. They took away the financial burden to leave Louise and me to concentrate on the children.

We nearly broke up. It took Lou a while to get round the fact that I'd been lying to her. The stress and the lies took their toll on us. We became less romantic. We found it more difficult to communicate our feelings to each other. But the trust is returning, and I'm trying so hard not to gamble again. Fatherhood is the most amazing thing that's ever happened to me. The only thing that really gives me confidence now is my children. Walking down the street with my son and daughter beats any other feeling. At last, I know what's really important in life.

Fifteen

ONE HIT WONDER

The turmoil at Carlisle continued into the 2001/02 campaign. Every season there was a huge turnover of players and a different manager, sometimes more than one. When Dario Gradi reached his 1,000th match as Crewe manager, the *Daily Telegraph* worked out how many managers every other Football League and Premiership club had had during his reign. For once, Carlisle were top of the table: there had been eighteen managers in eighteen years at Brunton Park.

The latest was Roddy Collins, brother of former world boxing champion Steve. Roddy had taken charge for 2001/02 but was frustrated by the same regime which had pushed out Ian Atkins. Collins could only afford players no one else wanted and he could only give them short-term contracts. It was no surprise to see Carlisle in their fourth consecutive fight for League survival. The fans were in despair. This was on an internet message board: 'I don't believe in fairytales any more, there are no more Jimmy Glass's in the crystal ball. We are slowly bleeding to death and there is little life left in us. All this because of one fat greedy bastard... When the last person switches off the lights at Brunton Park we will have lost everything, never to return.'

The only constant factor through all these struggles was the owner. The first AGM for two years was dominated by Michael Knighton. When Roddy Collins invited questions from shareholders the first person to stand up was Knighton. He asked why Carlisle United were struggling at the bottom of the League. The answer was painfully obvious to everyone except him.

In January 2002 it seemed a saviour had arrived. Dublin businessman John Courtenay was a friend of Roddy Collins. Collins explained Carlisle's potential and Courtenay agreed to meet Michael Knighton. Knighton, of course, was desperate to sell; Courtenay wanted to buy.

But when weeks of talks broke down, Courtenay made the same claims as previous potential buyers: just as a deal was almost done, Knighton moved the goalposts. Things which had been agreed as part of the deal were suddenly excluded; things which had never been mentioned before suddenly became vital parts of any sale.

Despite all the problems, Roddy Collins secured Carlisle's Division Three safety with a few games to spare. He was then sacked by Mark Knighton, supposedly for criticising the board. Collins and John Courtenay were inseparably linked. With Collins out of the picture, so was Courtenay. The future looked bleak once again. Carlisle had debts of more than £2 million and were banned from signing players. The club had to beg the PFA for a loan to pay wages. Nearly 16,000 people signed a petition calling for a change of ownership. Fans boycotted the last home game of the season and marched around Brunton Park to protest against Michael Knighton.

Knighton responded to the fans' concerns by vowing to close Carlisle United. Knighton told the chairman of CCUIST that he would withdraw the club from the Football League and ask if another team could be promoted from the Conference to take Carlisle's place. If the League refused, he would fulfil the next season's fixtures with YTS kids. He said the people of Cumbria didn't deserve a Football League team. He would board up Brunton Park and put up posters saying CCUIST killed the club by insulting the Knighton family. Fans could march around the ground as often as they liked but all they would see would be weeds growing. He said he had discussed it with his family and they had told him to throw the keys to Brunton Park in the river. Knighton again claimed his wife and children had been abused. But even if that was true, he put them in the firing line by giving them jobs at the club – and then by claiming that the decision to withdraw from the League was theirs as much as his.

It seemed my goal had been just a stay of execution. I had saved Carlisle United only for the club's owner to destroy it. Although there was intense anger in Cumbria, people were very jaded about what could be done to get rid of Knighton. The past few years had destroyed a lot of fight and belief. But nothing is impossible. If I'd saved Carlisle once, why couldn't I help do it again? I couldn't come up for a last-minute corner, but there must be something I could do.

I spent a lot of time making phone calls and taking advice from business people. I asked around in Cumbria and heard about Brian Scowcroft, an insurance tycoon and one of the richest men in the county. I rang him and he invited me up for a chat. I took Dick Young of CCUIST along with me and we put the masterplan to Brian over a pub lunch. I knew he had the means and I tried to give him the motive. He owns a business park on the outskirts of Carlisle and I suggested that Carlisle United could move there. We could bring in Peter Beardsley as manager and give the people of Carlisle something to throw their weight behind. Brian listened, but he didn't go for it. I never really felt he took me seriously. He was used to dealing with businessmen and I was just a footballer who was getting a bit excited.

Carlisle's MP raised the club's plight in the House of Commons again. A few weeks after Knighton's threat, the Inland Revenue, who were owed more than £500,000, issued the club with a winding-up order. Carlisle United went into voluntary administration in an attempt to fend off their creditors. For the first time in ten years the club was not controlled by the Knightons. Potential buyers gathered, including John Courtenay. After a summer of negotiation he emerged as the new owner. Michael Knighton was gone at last, with a lot more than the £75,000 he had paid for Carlisle. But the bad smell lingered on.

It emerged that Knighton's company had charged cash-strapped Carlisle £225,000 in 'management fees' during his final year at Brunton Park. His son Mark had borrowed thousands of pounds from the club, interest free. The club's new auditors said there had been no reliable system for recording cash takings at the turnstiles. Much of Carlisle United's history disappeared at the same time as the Knighton family. The walls had been stripped of photographs and memorabilia dating back nearly a century. Some were found in a skip outside the ground.

Brunton Park's first post-Knighton match was a wonderful day. Thirteen thousand fans turned up for the visit of Hartlepool on 10 August. On the pitch before the game John Courtenay presented me with life membership of Carlisle United. It was a long way from my previous visit to Brunton Park when I'd struggled to get a ticket.

After the game I was introduced to an old man who had only a few weeks to live. I took him out on the pitch and we re-enacted my goal in front of the empty stands. He could hardly kick the ball but he managed to knock it into the net at the second attempt. I hope that moment meant even a fraction to him of what it meant to me.

Courtenay reinstalled Roddy Collins as manager, but 2002/03 was another hard season. As part of the takeover deal the administrator had set Courtenay a strict budget, so Carlisle started the season with only a handful of professionals and struggled throughout. On Easter Monday, Carlisle lost 6-1 at Wrexham. With three games left they looked like dropping out of the League, especially as this was the first season when two clubs fell into the Conference. The irony of Carlisle being relegated the season after Michael Knighton left would have been unbelievably cruel. I dreaded my goal becoming a curiosity instead of something that really mattered.

After losing at Wrexham, Carlisle had two more away games, at Torquay and Shrewsbury. They won them both. They were safe again, by one point. I don't know what's more amazing, the fact that Carlisle keep getting into these situations or that they keep getting out of them. In 1987 Burnley escaped relegation to the Conference on the final day of the season; fifteen years later they were on the verge of the Premiership. It would give me so much satisfaction to see Carlisle capitalise on my goal in a similar way.

I don't believe in destiny, but sometimes I think about the trail of coincidence which led to the goal and I wonder how so many pieces fell into place. If Richard Knight hadn't been recalled by Derby, Carlisle wouldn't have needed me. If Plymouth's Paul Gibbs hadn't broken his leg, Carlisle's last game would have finished at the same time as Scarborough's and we wouldn't have known that we could still stay up. If Scarborough had won it would all have been academic. If I hadn't run up the pitch; if the ball hadn't fallen at my feet... I know it sounds strange, but I feel as if football rewarded me for my love of the game, and for having the balls to go to Carlisle in the first place. I didn't put in enough work to have a glittering career. But football gave me that moment.

I still think about it every day. It's in my face all the time, in the photograph on my wall, in the reaction when I meet someone new. It's a JFK moment. Everyone remembers where they were, how they heard, what they did. I'll always be known as the goalscoring goalkeeper. I'll always be a pub-quiz question.

My description of the goal earlier in this book is based on the videos and the press cuttings. I know what happened because I've watched it a thousand times. Millions of people around the world saw it. But the one person who should have been able to explain the goal can't remember it. I cannot remember what it felt like to strike the ball. It was sitting there in front of me and...

I've stared at the photographs. I've watched the replay in slow motion over and over again. I've sat there with the remote control and tried to relive it. To remember just a split second, to recapture the feeling I had, would be worth millions to me. But I can't do it. When I remember it now, it's like I'm looking down on myself. I see it the way everyone else does because I've watched it so many times. I think, 'Was that me? Did I do that?' That taught me something. You've got to enjoy life while it's there because even the greatest moments don't last.

Sometimes I think about what would have happened if I'd missed. I see images, as clear as anything, of the goalkeeper making a save or the ball hitting a defender on the shin and bouncing out. It scares the life out of me. Sometimes I think, 'What if I hadn't scored but I'd saved a penalty?' or, 'What if I'd dropped a cross and we'd been relegated?' I've imagined every scenario, and realised that nothing can compare with what actually happened.

Even now I get calls from newspapers, magazines, radio stations and television companies. When I was at Kingstonian a journalist came over from Holland to interview me. He sent me the magazine, which included a six-page feature but no translation. 'Jimmy Glass stond op de rand van zijn zestienmetergebied en keek naar zijn trainer,' as they say in Holland.

In 2002 my goal was number seventy-two in Channel 4's *The 100 Greatest Sporting Moments*. It was the only incident from English football's lower three divisions to make the list out of the hundreds of thousands of matches which have been played there for more than a century. That same year, two singles were released within a few weeks of each other by bands at opposite ends of the country. One song was called 'Jimmy Glass' and the other 'The Eighth of May'. There's also a band in Yorkshire called Jimmy Glass. In the past year I've been interviewed by an artist who's making a documentary about football and I've heard about a writer who wants to do a play based on the goal. I don't know how long the fascination will last. It might be a lifetime. The consequences are still obvious every day, at least to Carlisle and Scarborough fans.

There was an interview in the *Sun* with former Rushden striker Mark Sale, who was talking about his fight against cancer. He said, 'I was on loan to Plymouth when the Carlisle goalie Jimmy Glass scored that last-minute goal against us that kept them in the League. So I'm well aware miracles CAN happen.' Maybe they can. I discovered that one of the Archbishop of Canterbury's aides was a Carlisle supporter. The night before my goal he asked the Archbishop to pray for his team.

For a couple of years I couldn't understand why I wasn't treated with more respect by people in football. If I ever mentioned it in the dressing room, or if a fan sent me a letter, it was, 'Living off your goal again, are you?' I sat down with Rodney Marsh one day. We were talking about legendary players, and I said, 'How do you define a legend? I'm struggling to understand. Am I a legend?'

'No,' he said. 'You're not a legend. But your goal is legendary.'

I was happy with that. I finally understood. Whatever happens, I will always be remembered for a legendary sporting moment. I'm part of it but it's not about me. It's about that split-second when the impossible happened.

I'm two people now. Most days I'm James Glass, an IT salesman in Dorset who's trying to get his life together. No one knows me from Adam. But in Carlisle I walk through the streets with my head down, scared of making eye contact in case someone starts shouting my name. Up there it's a different world and I'm a different person. The only thing people know about is that one moment. It doesn't matter how much of me gets chipped away in the meantime. I come to Cumbria and it's 8 May 1999 all over again.

It seems everyone has a photograph of my goal on their wall. These days I pose for pictures with children who weren't even born when I scored. I never get tired of talking about it. The four-yard toe-ender has now become an overhead kick from the halfway line.

People ask me to ring their friends or partners and say hello. One man explained that he was in trouble with his girlfriend. She had asked him what the best day of his life was, expecting him to say the day they met; he told her it was when I scored. This bloke asked me to call her and say he was only joking. 'Hello,' I said. 'He was just kidding about my goal. And he says he loves you very much.'

He started shaking his head and mouthing, 'Don't say that!'

'Er, no – he doesn't love you,' I added.

He grinned and gave me a thumbs-up. Northerners – you've got to love them.

If I feel down all I need to do is head north and I'm treated like a king. I can't buy the look on people's faces when I walk into a room. If my family was homeless I could knock on any door in Carlisle and they'd take us in. That thought has kept me going for the past few years. I need those fans now as much as they needed me that afternoon when I ran up the pitch. All the praise is a great ego boost, but it's dangerous. I could start believing it.

For my first two years as an IT salesman I still felt like a footballer. I was torn between being a footballer and a salesman without really being either. I was in Dorset but my head was always somewhere else. When my life had settled down and the clouds of gambling had cleared, a question began to nag away at me: why aren't I playing any more? My football career felt like a half-finished story. I could never regret scoring the goal, but it was eating away at me that I wanted to be respected as a goalkeeper as well. Instead of selling computer upgrades I wanted to sell something I really believed in – the idea of myself as a 'keeper. Not doing the thing I excel at was driving me mad. I couldn't even enjoy Sunday morning matches because I felt I was selling myself short every time I ran out. There were still things to prove.

I had the idea of spending six months training at Brunton Park to regain my fitness before looking for a club. In return I would do PR work for Carlisle United, visiting schools and helping to attract sponsors. This time I would really focus on football, working harder, eating better, fulfilling my potential. Has anyone returned to professional football after sitting behind a desk for two years? I thought it would be a great achievement to come back from that, after the mess my life had been in. My goal was a fluke, but this would be something I could really take pride in.

I discussed the idea with John Courtenay. John thought it would jeopardise my relationship with the club and the fans if I was in Carlisle all the time. I don't hold that against him. He's a businessman and he made a business decision. Bringing me back to Carlisle was a gamble that could have gone wrong for him. So now I have to put my football career to bed and work out what to do with my life.

I didn't want my career to end with a whimper instead of a bang, but it's not the end of the world. I'm still trying to find a way of using the goal to help my family, and then I'll need to put it away. I was watching an FA Cup tie on television between Hereford and Wrexham. At half-time they interviewed Ronnie Radford and Ricky George about the goals they scored for Hereford against Newcastle thirty years earlier. I turned to Louise and said, 'Will you promise me something?'

'What?'

'If I'm on the telly in thirty years' time talking about my goal, shoot me.'

In April 2003 I was a guest of Carlisle United when they reached the LDV Vans Trophy final at Cardiff's Millennium Stadium. After the match dozens of Carlisle fans were crowding around me for auto-graphs and photographs. One man turned to Louise and said, 'Alan Ross would be turning in his grave.' Alan Ross is a former Carlisle goalkeeper who played more times for the club than anyone else. The man at Cardiff was probably right. Alan Ross made 500 appearances over fifteen years; I ran up the pitch once and swung my leg at the ball. It's strange, even to me.

But some things make more sense now. Since entering the 'real world' I understand football much better. Now I know that people make bad decisions everywhere. That's not just football, it's life. Since becoming a dad I've realised how many of my problems were down to my immaturity. And there's one thing football taught me, and deep down I still believe it: anything is possible – absolutely anything.

EPILOGUE

Carlisle United struggled yet again during the 2003/04 season. The club lost their first five matches and Roddy Collins was sacked. His replacement was Paul Simpson, a Carlisle-born midfielder who took the job of player/manager. The club was still strait-jacketed by debts from the Knighton era. The administrator appointed by the Knighton family had arranged for the club to pay back every penny of its debt. Most clubs in Carlisle's situation pay no more than fifty per cent. The administrator also charged John Courtenay nearly £500,000.

Paul Simpson was unable to strengthen his squad until November 2003, when the financial restrictions were finally lifted. Simpson then brought in several experienced players. They were desperately needed. On 20 December, Carlisle kicked off their home game against Torquay sixteen points adrift of safety. Their first twenty-one League matches had yielded a grand total of five points: there had been one win, two draws and eighteen defeats.

The next twenty-three games produced 39 points. The football world watched the revival in disbelief. A team which had just set a club record of twelve consecutive League defeats embarked on half a season of promotion form. By the end of April, Carlisle had given themselves another shot at survival.

On 24 April the Cumbrians were winning 3-2 at Mansfield when they conceded an injury-time penalty. If Mansfield scored, Carlisle were in the Conference. Carlisle goalkeeper Matty Glennon made a superb save to keep his team alive.

The following Saturday, Carlisle played Cheltenham at home and needed another win to sustain their survival hopes. Carlisle took an early lead and held it until five minutes from full time. Then Cheltenham's Kayode Odejayi headed an equaliser at the Waterworks End goal where Jimmy Glass had scored five years earlier. Carlisle's seventy-six-year stay in the Football League was over. Jimmy sat on the steps of the Paddock with his head in his hands. Carlisle's last League game was a 1-0 defeat at Doncaster on 8 May; the date known to Carlisle fans as St Jimmy's Day.

During the next few weeks there was speculation that Carlisle might win a reprieve from relegation, as their Division Three rivals Darlington were in danger of being declared bankrupt. Darlington owed more than £20 million, but in May 2004 their administrator arranged for the club to write off more than ninety-nine per cent of its debts. If Carlisle had enjoyed the same terms, John Courtenay would have had to pay creditors less than £20,000.

However, Carlisle's prospects look far brighter than if the club had been relegated during Jimmy's time there in 1999. Only one club was promoted from the Conference then; now two go up. In May 2004 Shrewsbury became the first relegated League club in fourteen years to bounce back at the first attempt.

Jimmy and Louise got married in Poole, Dorset, in January 2004.

Jimmy was still working at Spire, and playing as a forward for Spire Broadway in the Bournemouth Sunday League, when, in February, Bournemouth Sports of the Dorset Premier League asked him to go in goal for them. 'The adrenaline started pumping when I pulled the gloves on again and I got the desire to play at the highest level I could,' said Jimmy. He resigned his job and attempted to become a goalkeeper again. He started training with Bournemouth and in March he played three games for Weymouth in the Dr Martens Premier League.

In July Jimmy played two pre-season matches for East Sussex club Lewes, of the Conference South. Lewes then withdrew their offer of a contract, and Jimmy relapsed into gambling. He has joined Gamblers Anonymous and is working as a taxi driver in Dorset while considering his next move.

In April 2004 Jimmy was in goal for Bournemouth Sports' last game of the season, at home to Hamworthy. Bournemouth Sports were trailing 1-0 when they won a last-minute corner. Jimmy abandoned his goal and ran upfield, for the first time since scoring for Carlisle. 'I legged it up the pitch and reached the penalty area just in time for another moment of glory – and our player took a short corner! He said he hadn't noticed me. I was the only man on the pitch wearing red, our manager had been shouting, 'Go on, Jimmy!', and he hadn't noticed me. Unbelievable...'

APPENDIX
Career Statistics of Jimmy Glass

CAREER

Chelsea; trials 1987
Crystal Palace; schoolboy 1988, apprentice 1989, professional 1991
Dulwich Hamlet; on loan January-May 1990
Carshalton; on loan 1990-1991
Portsmouth; on loan February-April 1995
Gillingham; on loan December 1995-January 1996
Burnley; on loan January-February 1996
AFC Bournemouth; free transfer March 1996
Swindon Town; free transfer June 1998
Carlisle United; on loan April-May 1999
Cambridge United; signed February 2000
Crystal Palace; trained with March 2000
Brentford; signed March 2000
Wimbledon; trained with July 2000
Exeter City; trials July 2000
Crawley Town; signed July 2000
Oxford United; signed August 2000
Brentford; trained with February 2001
Crawley Town; signed February 2001
Kingstonian; signed February 2001
Yeovil Town; trials July 2001
Brentford; trained with July 2001
Brockenhurst; signed August 2001
Spire Technology, Dorset; IT salesman August 2001-February 2004
Salisbury City; signed September 2001
AFC Bournemouth; trained with February-May 2004
Weymouth; signed March 2004
Lewes; signed July 2004

APPEARANCES

Football League: 114
FA Cup: 4
League Cup: 5
Auto Windscreens Shield/LDV Vans Trophy: 8

INDEX

Graham, George 103, 126
Granville, John 105, 140
Gray, Andy 20, 29
Grays Athletic FC 23
Greenwich Borough FC 28
Griffin, Johnny 113
Grimsby Town FC 68-9
Gudjohnsen, Eidur 58
Guttulsrod, Clas Andre 121

Halifax Town FC 86
Hamworthy FC 156
Harris, Mark 129
Hartlepool United FC 9, 86
Hatton, Derek 117
Hawking, Stephen 74
Hednesford FC 129-30
Hendon FC 23
Henry, Thierry 48
Hereford United FC 154
Heritage, Paul 83
Higgins, John 47
Hoddle, Glenn 45, 103
Holland, Matty 62, 65
Hopper, Tony 89
Horley FC 17
Hoult, Russell 85
Howe, Eddie 65
Hucker, Peter 26
Huddersfield Town FC 108
Hull City FC 53, 83
Humphrey, John 45

Icke, David 121
Ilkeston Town FC 108
Ince, Paul 45
Ipswich Town FC 55, 79

Jansen, Matt 84
Johnson, Gary 138
Jones, Vinny 75
Juventus FC 19, 82

Kassam, Firoz 120
Keane, Roy 44, 114
Keegan, Kevin 66
Kember, Steve 40
Kemp, David 38, 122, 126
Kettering Town FC 142
Kingstonian FC 129-35
Kinnear, Joe 121
Knight, Alan 43, 44
Knight, Richard 85, 119, 120, 138

Knighton, Mark 123, 137, 149
Knighton, Michael 84-5, 89, 93, 94, 98, 99-101, 117-8, 123-5, 137, 147-9

Lampard, Frank 102
Lara, Brian 47
Law, Denis 83
Leeds United FC 51, 84
Leicester City FC 126
Lewes FC 156
Lewington, Ray 46, 50
Lewis, Alan 61, 62
Leyton Orient FC 46
Liege FC 47-8
Little, Glen 27
Liverpool FC 14, 19, 22
Lynam, Des 97

Macari, Lou 109
Machin, Mel 51, 53, 55-7, 64, 65-6, 67, 140, 143
Maidstone United FC 61
Manchester City FC 83
Manchester United FC 9, 30, 31-2
Mansfield Town FC 155
Marsh, Rodney 118-9, 152
Marshall, Andy 56-7, 58
Marshall, Shaun 111
Martlew, Eric 125
Martyn, Nigel 22, 31, 44, 51
Massey, Stuart 38
Maxwell, Robert 119
McCall, Steve 89
McClellan, Ross 75
McCoist, Ally 103
McDermott, John 69
McFarland, Roy 110, 111-2
McMahon, Steve 73, 75-6, 95
Merson, Paul 58
Middlemass, Clive 51
Middlesbrough FC 85
Millwall FC 70, 73
Mincher, Keith 101
Morecambe FC 130
Morgan, Piers 96
Mullen, Jimmy 50-1
Murdoch, Stuart 118

Nash, Carlo 51
Newcastle United FC 84
Nicholas, Peter 46

Nimmo, Keith 15
Noades, Ron 20-1, 29, 46, 51, 113-4
Northwich Victoria FC 131
Norwich City FC 56-7
Ndah, George 32, 110

Odejayi, Kayode 155
O' Driscoll, Sean 59
Oldham Athletic FC 37
Onuora, Iffy 110
O'Reilly, Gary 28, 65, 67-8
Owen, Michael 131
Oxford United FC 119-23, 126, 127

Pardew, Alan 18
Paxman, Jeremy 103
Pearcey, Jason 113, 114
Pearson, Nigel 85-9, 92, 93, 101, 120
Pennington, Vic 15
Peterborough United FC 86, 89, 91, 115
Perry, Chris 16
Perry, Fred 33
Phillips, Lee 89
Plymouth Argyle FC 66, 86, 89-92, 106, 138, 150
Poom, Mart 85
Portsmouth FC 43-4, 46
Port Vale FC 44

Queens Park Rangers FC 31, 46
Quinn, Jimmy 76-7, 78-9, 81, 95, 96, 105, 106, 107-8, 109, 122, 140

Radford, Ronnie 154
Raynes Park Rovers FC 15, 16, 129, 142
Reading FC 18
River Plate FC 33
Rolling, Franck 67, 69
Ross, Alan 154
Rushden and Diamonds FC 100
Russell, John 97, 133
Ryder, Steve 91

Sabatini, Gabriela 32-3
Salako, John 29, 37
Sale, Mark 152

If you are interested in purchasing
other books published by Tempus, or in case you have
difficulty finding any Tempus books in your local bookshop,
you can also place orders directly through our website

www.tempus-publishing.com